Creative Landscaping

Creative Landscaping

IDEAS, DESIGNS, AND BLUEPRINTS

Derek Fell

FRIEDMAN/FAIRFAX
PUBLISHERS

A FRIEDMAN/FAIRFAX BOOK

© 1995 by Michael Friedman Publishing Group, Inc.

Library of Congress Cataloging-in-Publication Data

Fell, Derek.
    Creative landscaping : ideas, designs, and blueprints / Derek
Fell.
        p.   cm.
    Rev. ed. of: Home landscaping / Elizabeth Murray and Derek Fell.
New York : Simon and Schuster , 1988.
    Includes bibliographical references (p.   ) and index.
    ISBN 1-56799-156-4
    1. Landscape architecture. 2. Landscape gardening. I. Murray,
Elizabeth, date, Home landscaping.   II Title.
    [SB473.M869   1995]
    712'.6—dc20   94-26765
                                                            CIP

Editor: Tim Frew
Art Director: Jeff Batzli
Designer: Robert W. Kosturko
Photography Editors: Christopher C. Bain and Emilya Naymark

Originally published as *Home Landscaping: Ideas, Styles, and Designs for Creative Outdoor Spaces*

Typeset by B.P.E. Graphics, Inc.
Color separations by Hong Kong Scanner Craft Company, Ltd.
Printed in China by Leefung-Asco Printers Ltd.

For bulk purchases and special sales, please contact:
Friedman/Fairfax Publishers
Attention: Sales Department
15 West 26th Street
New York, NY 10010
212/685-6610 FAX 212/685-1307

DEDICATION

To O.D. Gallagher, who taught me to write, Harry Smith, who taught me to photograph gardens, and Hiroshi Makita, who taught me how to see gardens as works of art.

ACKNOWLEDGMENTS

Many thanks to all those garden owners and landscape architects who allowed me to photograph their gardens, especially Ruth Levitan, Jack Miller, Carter Van Dyke, Lyddon Pennock, Marshall Brickman, Earl Jamison, James Hester, Matthew Drozd, Emily Whaley, Garrett Eckbo, Ed Toth, Tom Hallowell, and Esteban Vicente. Special thanks to Elizabeth Murray for the text to chapters one, two, four, six, seven, eight, nine, and the appendix. I provided the outline and all the photography and captions, and wrote chapters three and five. I would also like to thank Kathy Nelson, my administrative assistant; Wendy Fields, my grounds supervisor at Cedaridge Farm, where I work and garden; and my wife, Carolyn, for all their help in making this project possible.

CONTENTS

INTRODUCTION

People are often confused by the idea of landscape design. A dictionary definition of landscaping is "to adorn or improve a section of ground by contouring the land and planting ...." Just as any home, regardless of size, must be carefully planned for optimum use of space, so can a landscape be designed. There are aspects of landscape design which can be done either through the services of a qualified professional or as a "do-it-yourself" project. But even if you choose to rely heavily on the services of a design professional, such as a landscape architect, contractor, or designer, it still pays to have a fundamental knowledge of landscape design to enable you to communicate your ideas and desires.

Many of the most successful landscape designs rely primarily on the owner's involvement, with the help of professionals to polish up ideas or supervise construction details. In fact, any attempt at landscape design can end in fiasco unless the owner shows enthusiastic input into the project, for it is only the owner who can determine how much time can be devoted to continuing maintenance. If the owner's time is restricted and no one else is available to spend time watering, feeding, and pruning, then the landscape may need to be drought-tolerant and labor-saving, with more emphasis on "hardscaping" (brick, stone, gravel, and wood) rather than "softscaping" (plants). However, if the owner has the time and enthusiasm, then the landscape designer can be adventurous and place a heavier emphasis on plants—introducing beds of flowering annuals, drifts of flowering bulbs, borders of perennials, collections of flowering shrubs, and skyline effects using deciduous trees that turn color and drop their leaves in the autumn. A beautiful home landscape increases property values, which is the main objective for many homeowners—choosing special projects, such as an attractive driveway or entrance planting, to maximize their investment. For many other homeowners, however, a garden provides so much pleasure that maintenance and cost become unimportant—the garden comes to be appreciated simply as a source of relaxation, pride, and a sense of well-being.

The first step in any landscaping project is to assess your needs. How will the landscape be used and by whom? Will it be an extension of the house itself, used for entertaining, dining, and relaxing? Is it a priority to have pleasant views and vistas from inside the house? Are there children who will play in the garden or an avid gardener to happily tend flower beds? When will the garden mostly be used—days, evenings, summers, or the year round? Each function requires different design and various amounts of time and money for maintenance.

The next step is to establish the "bones" or structure of the landscape. The walkways, tree placement, shrub layout, any construction such as decks, patios, and water features create the skeleton, the framework that holds the design integrity and interest year-round. The framework also helps to establish the layout of the garden. The planting of annual color embellishes the bone structure. The addition of garden ornaments such as small statues, garden furniture, containers, and lanterns are accents that personalize and enhance the garden, enriching the area with focus and style. The addition of a particular style of gazebo or entrance gate, for example, can establish the sense of a Victorian or Oriental garden more successfully than plants alone.

Unfortunately, there is a notion that good landscape design is synonymous with lavish plantings and that if a garden is not ablaze with floral color for most of the year, it is a failure. That is not necessarily so. In fact, the very best examples of Japanese landscape design rely very little on floral color; the essentials of a dramatic Japanese landscape are trees, water, stone, and evergreens. Symbolism, composition, texture, and form all take precedence over color in a Japanese garden. Where color is introduced, it tends to be subdued for seasonal effect and is never garish.

The Japanese are masters of simplicity, understatement, structure, and serenity in the garden. Their gardens have movement (water, paths, raked gravel, etc.) and spaces that encourage contemplation. They can be adapted to a very small area or a large landscape. The "bone structure" is clearly defined using a strong sense of balance and proportion throughout the design.

Introducing designed space into the landscape can ensure that a garden is used for a multitude of functions. There is a myriad of landscape professionals—garden designers, landscape designers, landscape architects, and landscape contractors—who can help design and install gardens. It is important to understand their differences in order to distinguish between their expertise and your needs.

Frederick Law Olmsted (the person responsible for landscaping New York City's picturesque Central Park) is credited with coining the term "landscape architect" to describe a person who professionally performs the function of altering and planting the land. At the time it was a controversial name because "landscaping" and "architecture" seemed to be contradictions —landscaping concerned natural elements like soil and plants, while architecture was considered to be the art and science of designing and erecting buildings, which frequently destroyed the landscape. However, the design and placement of buildings in a garden setting can be an important landscape feature, particularly structures such as summerhouses, gazebos, temples, and boathouses. Ever since Olmsted married the words *landscape* and *architecture,* the word architecture has become more loosely defined as "any design or orderly arrangement perceived by man," but the definition of a landscape architect still confuses many people.

Legally and conceptually there are differences between a garden designer, landscape designer, landscape architect, and landscape contractor. A garden designer or landscape designer can be anyone who designs outdoor spaces—even a homeowner who scribbles out ideas on scraps of paper and hands them over to others to implement. Whether a person is called a *garden* designer or a *landscape* designer is often a matter of semantics, though garden designers tend to place a greater emphasis on plants, while landscape designers work more with durable materials such as redwood, brick, paving, and gravel.

Landscape architects must be licensed by the state or province. To qualify as a landscape architect in the state of California, for example, requires at least three years of training under a landscape architect, a four-year degree, and the passing of both written and oral examinations covering the legalities and history of landscape architecture, design, construction, and plant materials.

A landscape contractor, on the other hand, is the state-licensed person who physically moves the earth and does the construction—like a building contractor. This is the person with the bulldozer, the backhoe, and the labor to transform blueprints executed by a landscape architect into beautiful vistas, contoured berms, stone terraces, and other design elements.

How to choose a designer:

- recommendations from friends
- inquire who designed the gardens you admire locally
- look at photographs of candidates' previous work, or—if possible—visit a few of their gardens
- ask for references from past clients and check them out

This book addresses itself primarily to the homeowner who needs a clear understanding of the principles involved in landscape design. It will help this homeowner to formulate some clear concepts and communicate them intelligently to a landscape architect or landscape contractor. This is not so much a "how-to-do-it" book for the do-it-yourself enthusiast who wants to know how to design a bridge with a high arch, drain a swampy area, or install a flight of steps using landscape ties. Rather, it is a book that attempts to define some important design features for a stimulating home landscape. Particularly, it is a book of landscaping *ideas*—explaining why certain ideas work and showing how to apply them to specific garden settings.

chapter one:

ENTERTAINING AND RECREATION

ENTERTAINING

usually includes other people—having

friends over to enjoy drinks in the garden or

a barbecue on the terrace. Recreation, on

the other hand, includes group activities

such as volleyball and water sports, as well

as the more peaceful pastimes of sunbath-

ing, reading, and puttering in the garden.

Because of noise, active recreation should

be located away from the house.

DINING AREAS

A blanket on the lawn is a lovely way to picnic, but areas such as terraces, decks, and patios are more fitting for gracious dining. Sites off the living room, kitchen, or dining room provide easy access to the house. When designing a terrace or deck, make it strong enough to accommodate garden furniture and containers of seasonal color and large enough to allow people to circulate easily. A terrace should be at least 6 inches (15 centimeters) lower than the house to be protected from the weather. Broad steps provide a comfortable transition and become welcome sitting areas. A Thomas Church formula for well-proportioned outdoor steps and stairs is:

A screened-in porch serves as an extension of the living room where the owners can enjoy outdoor dining and entertaining without being bothered by insects. This simple design was built on an existing brick terrace. The roof is clear, corrugated fiberglass with a slight pitch for drainage. The siding is constructed of panels of wire screening stretched across a frame of two-by-fours.

"twice the riser plus the tread equals 26 inches (66 centimeters)." If, for example, the grade dictates 6-inch (15-centimeter) risers (the raised part of a step), the tread (flat part where your feet step) should be 14 inches (36 centimeters). Each step should have about a quarter-inch (6-millimeter) pitch to allow for drainage. Building materials depend on the owner or designer's preference, the overall palette of the area, and the design. All-weather materials such as large, flat stones (with tight, well-filled mortar), brick, or poured cement work well in many situations. (Refer to Chapter 4 under walkway surfaces for advantages and disadvantages of various materials.) A level, well-drained surface will be appreciated for years to come when furniture

doesn't wobble, water doesn't puddle, and shoe heels don't catch on loose joints. Raised flower beds, retaining walls, and low railings around the terrace or deck can be used for extra seating if the copings are 18 to 24 inches (46 to 61 centimeters) wide.

A deciduous shade tree is also a welcome addition. Consider a Japanese cherry or crabapple for its blossoms and colorful foliage; an Albizia (silk tree) for its delicate foliage, summer bloom, and umbrella shading ability; or a honey locust for its pretty shade patterns and overhead tracery. If insects are a nuisance, create a screened-in porch or gazebo. Cool breezes will blow through, light will shine in, and the view will be visible, but pests will be kept out.

A raised terrace (left) extends directly out from the dining room, taking advantage of the roof overhang. The stone flower bed creates an attractive transition. Below: This tiled patio is located off the kitchen door and serves as a dining area as well as a breezeway between the garage and the house. The canvas roof can be adjusted to suit the weather.

OFFICE SETTINGS

Nothing is more pleasant and relaxing than a quiet reprieve in a garden. An office that looks onto a fresh, green garden rests the eyes and spirit from the daily demands of a busy workday.

Many office gardens are designed just for viewing. The sight of various shades and textures of green is refreshing, and if the use of flowers is limited to one or two colors, they will not be distracting. A small wall fountain, with water cascading into a tiny pool, or a modest jardiniere will create the soothing sound of falling water and be much appreciated after the noise of telephones, typewriters, and computers.

If space permits, a small terrace, which can be used for eating lunch or talking with a client, is a welcome addition. Privacy is as important a consideration as easy access and can be accomplished by screens, hedges, walls, or fences. Garden access for clients, deliveries, and visitors can be clearly marked by paths and/or attractive signs. An office garden can be on a rooftop, an entrance deck, or an inner courtyard. It may be visible from only one direction or from all sides or even from above. The design must take into account the garden's multiple purposes, its visibility, the traffic flow, and available maintenance.

In today's big city buildings many office gardens are completely indoors. Interior landscape design has become a very sophisticated and specialized art. Some buildings boast plantings two to three stories high, creating bamboo, fern, or ficus forests. Wherever the setting, an office garden can increase the pleasure and productivity of employees and clients alike.

Garrett Eckbo, a landscape architect from Berkeley, California, converted his detached garage into an office. He took up the existing driveway and installed a brick patio and a container garden. To gain privacy from the road, as well as lost storage space, Eckbo designed an attractive tool shed made of recycled materials.

This fireplace/grill combination (left) is a functional and handsome garden feature. The redwood arbor and latticework create a cozy enclosure as well as a place to grow vines and display hanging plants. Below: An alternative design is built from an existing brick wall that surrounds a swimming pool. This design provides counter space for cooking and serving food.

BARBECUE AREAS

Throughout history, fire has both intrigued and drawn people. A fireplace placed in the garden for cooking and heat immediately becomes the center of social gathering. A barbecue of brick or stone can be built off the house chimney, and will add a cooking area to a terrace near the living room. If you have a pool, a fireplace and grill can be easily incorporated on the pool patio for entertaining. This is especially lovely for warm, summer evenings, enhanced by good exterior lighting, comfortable outdoor furniture, and a stereo system for music. Portable, wheeled grills and hibachis are less elaborate but are convenient and allow for more versatility.

CHILDREN'S PLAY SPACES

Children enjoy both "defined play" on objects like swings and slides, which have been designed for specific uses, and "creative play" in areas such as sandboxes where they use their imaginations to build castles, villages, roads, rivers, and bridges. A space that is designed to accommodate both types of play will stimulate children physically and mentally for hours. For example, a playhouse or tree fort becomes a school-house, lookout tower, or clubhouse for the child, and years later will still be a garden feature to be enjoyed by adults.

Plants in places where small children play should be non-poisonous and free of dangerous thorns. There are many plants that encourage play, imagination, and fan-

tasy. Hollyhock flowers, fuchsias, and snapdragons can be fashioned into dolls, ballerinas, and talking dragons. Sunflowers are fun to grow, eat, feed to birds or squirrels, and draw. Polebeans and scented flowering vines such as honeysuckle can be grown on teepees for children to sit inside. They will be able to feel the cool, green air and taste the honeysuckle nectar and fresh beans. A child's very own vegetable, strawberry, or flower patch is an ideal way to introduce basic botany and the love of gardening. Nature study can be encouraged by planting flowers and shrubs that will attract birds and butterflies. Putting up birdhouses, a birdbath, and feeders is also fun. A sundial will introduce children to the passing of time and the earth's rotation.

Multi-functional playsets are now very attractive and creative. They are constructed from either wood or metal and can be ordered through various mail-order cat-

alog firms. Installation is made easy by following manufacturer's instructions. Sand or tanbark make ideal mediums to jump into from swings and slides. Confining loose materials to the play area will always be difficult, but it helps to edge the area with wood or brick and recess it a few inches below ground level. Maintenance is very important for safety, so check regularly for loose bolts, sharp metal, splintering wood, and low levels of sand or tanbark. When designing the place in the overall landscape scheme for the children's play area, keep in mind the children's need for supervision and their potential noisiness. Also consider how the area can be converted when the children have outgrown it. The greatest single play space for a child is a large, low-growing, climbing tree. It provides shade, hiding places, and space for forts and swings, and will foster adventure and friendships.

*C*hildren's play spaces ideally include both "creative" play areas, where they use their imaginations, and "defined" play areas for specific activities. Left: *Lawns provide an ideal play surface while flowerbeds with bright paint-box colors create an attractive setting. Playhouses and tree forts provide years of make-believe and adventure.* Right: *A large tree with sturdy, well-spaced branches is ideal for a structure, but if unavailable, three smaller tree trunks can provide the base for a "polehouse."* Below: *Another possibility is a raised platform house with a sandbox or toy storage underneath. With careful design and construction, a treehouse can be an attractive garden feature.*

INCORPORATING THE SWIMMING POOL

Take complete advantage of solar energy by positioning the swimming pool so it is hit by as much sunlight as possible. This will extend the hours of use per day as well as lengthen the swimming season by several weeks. Attractive screens, evergreen hedges, fences, and walls add wind protection and privacy. If you need wind protection but also desire a view, install a glass or plexiglass wall. This will frame the view as well as increase nearby temperatures by five to ten degrees—perfect for sunbathing!

One way of incorporating a swimming pool into the landscape is to make it a beautiful garden feature or a naturalistic pool. The combination of stone edges such as slate or flagstone and a dark blue or black bottom* gives a stunning effect. A

*T*his classically designed bathhouse (left) serves as an ornamental accent at the end of a lap pool. Jets of water from the corners converge in the middle, creating an elegant fountain. Above: This small garden features a hot tub with a pergola, over which fragrant vines will be trained. Over time, the vines will hide the structure, creating a cool garden sanctuary.

Above right: A Japanese teahouse provides the inspiration for this low bathhouse silhouetted against a gray-green backdrop of sheared olive trees. Right: This jacuzzi spa is raised above the nearby informal swimming pool by a set of encircling stone steps.

*Not recommended for homes with small children, as objects are difficult to see at the pool bottom.

waterfall or stream that cascades into the pool from a rockery and a few choice boulders at the water's edge can create a woodland feeling and also provide a good perching spot.

Hot tubs and spas have become popular places for family and friends to gather, talk, and relax. If close to the pool, they provide a convenient place for swimmers to warm up and adults to supervise children. Paving materials should be skid proof, nonglaring, comfortable to bare feet, and clean. Good choices include redwood decking, tile, slate, flagstone, brick, or—most inexpensive and versatile—concrete. Cement is easily colored and textured with pebbles, rock salt, sand, leaf prints, shells, beach glass, etc. A sitting area near the shallow end avoids splashing from dives and facilitates watching younger children. Paving should be at least 4 feet (1.2 meters) wide around the pool edge before lawn or planting areas begin in order to prevent leaves from getting in the pool.

A storage area adjacent to a patio is screened off by a decorative white trellis. The white door is embellished with a bronze plaque.

GARDEN AREAS

For recreation in the garden it is most enjoyable to have a potting shed and/or greenhouse. Many happy hours can be spent on garden projects such as growing orchids, forcing specialty bulbs, making topiary animals, creating flowering moss baskets, training bonsai, raising cut flowers in winter, and propagating plants from cuttings and seed. Some of the most detailed and time consuming tasks become extremely rewarding and pleasurable when working with plants.

A small greenhouse or an attractively designed potting shed can be a garden feature that even doubles as an outdoor kitchen for entertaining. An overhead roof of transparent corrugated fiberglass provides for both filtered light and rain protection. Side walls can be made of glass, plexiglass, lattice, wire screen, or sliding fiberglass panels. This work space can be designed to convert into a useful "garden kitchen"—put a wet bar and small refrigerator under a counter for ice, cold drinks, snacks, and to keep bulbs cool. A deep sink, hosebib, easy-to-clean work counter and floor, open shelves, cupboards, and closed soil bins that fit under the counter will make space efficient and neat. An outdoor kitchen will save many trips to the house when entertaining, and it is a wonderful place to arrange cut flowers, prepare garden vegetables, and make container-plant arrangements for both indoors and outdoors.

A completely functional work space can be screened from view with hedges or lattice panels. It is best located near the tool storage and driveway for delivery of soil, pots, and supplies.

Left: *A city garden features raised beds for both edible plants and flowering ornamentals. Well-defined brick paths lead to a quiet area with a bench at the center of the garden.* Below: *A vine-covered iron gate leads into a long, narrow garden featuring herbs. A plan on page 140 shows how the space was allocated.*

chapter two

RELAXATION

ELAXATION

in a quiet garden provides soothing repose

after a hectic day. The peacefulness of be-

ing outside with fresh air and fragrant plants

and the communing with nature revitalizes

and refreshes nearly everyone. The garden

may be a condominium deck with potted

plants and a favorite chair, an inner-city

courtyard, a suburban lot turned Garden of

Eden, or a large estate with a multitude of

garden features, but each garden should be personal and comfortable to the owner. Somewhere there will be a place to sit with a drink or recline with a book for relaxation.

ROMANTIC SPOTS

It is hard to define a "romantic garden" since something perceived as romantic to one person may not be to another. It's easy to see that any kind of lush, verdant environment contributes more to a romantic atmosphere than a landscape that relies heavily on masses of durable materials like low evergreen ground covers, concrete paving, and redwood decks. Also, romantic gardens tend to have color that reaches high into the sky—climbing roses, honeysuckle, clematis, wisteria, or jasmine either supported by arbors and trellises or left to scramble up tall trees or shrubs.

Romantic spaces generally appear to be devoid of boundaries, or at least boundaries are carefully camouflaged. Anything that gives the appearance of antiquity tends to evoke romance—a rusting plough, trees draped in Spanish moss, stonework and tree trunks covered with algae, moss edging a stream, and cushions of thyme

Above: Decorated with a grapevine motif and painted in a soft, natural green, this cast iron bench adds a romantic highlight to a small, informal garden. Right: *A billowing profusion of plants in these perennial borders helps to disguise the boundaries of this terrace garden. An oversized oak bench provides the setting for a private moment of reflection.*

and pinks planted among flagstone.

Secret passages, ruins, reflecting pools, boat docks, thatched summerhouses, dovecotes filled with white fantail doves, fern glades, sleek white bridges with lots of filigree or trelliswork, a maze in which to play hide-and-seek—these are some of the more unusual devices that help to introduce romantic overtones to a garden.

Romance is created with an abundance of fragrant, old-fashioned, pastel-colored flowers, such as roses and lilacs overgrown with honeysuckle, jasmine, and wisteria, giving the feeling of "wild abandonment." In a secluded garden room, seating for two on a cushioned bench or covered swing provides a cozy place for romance. Walled-in gardens of brick or stone covered with vines and rock plants, or formed from clipped hedges provide the privacy for romance. Old statuary of young maidens, cupids, and angels placed in secluded niches will inspire lovers while strolling in the garden. A romantic garden is made up of curves; straight lines are used only when planted with lush, flowering growth that spills to soften them. A garden designed to be viewed at night may have plants with white flowers and grey foliage to reflect the silver light of the moon.

Above: A fragrant pathway of herbs leads to an English bench of curved teak set off against a brick wall. Left: A grassy path meanders among beds and borders planted with wildflowers, perennials, and flowering shrubs in a romantic woodland garden.

Below: In a shady nook, a bamboo unexpectedly sprouts water into a decorative urn. Right: Circular stepping-stones and trellis fencing help to create a transition from an open, sunny spot to a shady area.

OASES

A garden oasis is an unexpected, pleasant spot within a contrasting environment. If the weather is hot and the sun beats down harshly, a pergola, arbor, or lathhouse could be built or a canvas canopy could be installed for shade. Leafy trees planted on a lawn provide natural coolness. A true oasis has the presence of water, even if only the small, symbolic gesture of a bamboo spigot gently spilling water into a ceramic or stone urn.

If the landscape is quite wooded and in deep shade, a welcome oasis can be formed by cutting some branches and creating a small circle of warm sunlight. If the environment is bustling with the noise of cars and neighbors, a quiet, private sitting place, surrounded by the sounds of leaves rustling, wind chimes tinkling, birds singing, and the trickle or flow of water becomes an oasis of peaceful solitude. An oasis in the garden is a place remote from worldly pressures where you can become more in tune with nature and yourself.

Above left: *This wisteria-covered arbor with a pair of facing benches creates a welcome oasis of shade in an open, sunny garden.* Above right: *A circular pool becomes a quiet oasis when surrounded by blood-red impatiens set off against a windscreen by dark hedges and evergreen trees.* Left: *Blossoms of crabapple and dogwood are reflected in the pond of this woodland garden.*

GARDEN ROOMS

Garden rooms can be either direct extensions of the house or completely separate structures that beckon visitors into the garden. They are commonly constructed from wood, metal, glass, screens, or brick, but can also be created with trimmed hedges or trees. The most romantic are hidden from direct view and must be "discovered" or "come upon" when exploring the garden. At Ladew Topiary Gardens in Maryland, Mr. Harvey S. Ladew was infamous for his romantic intentions. He would guide his chosen visitor on private walks in his garden, going from garden room to garden room. Hedges of various shapes and colors form the 22 different rooms, each with a completely different color scheme and theme. At the crest of the hill is the Greek temple of love with a statue of Venus. From the temple, the house is seen at the end of a great vista, framed by hedges shaped as waves with swans swimming on the crests. On the return to the house there is a delightful, eight-sided antique pavilion from England. Inside there is a tiny fireplace (what is more romantic on a chilly day?), a comfortable couch, and behind a gold-gilded mirror is a secret bar. Who wouldn't be completely enchanted?

A conservatory or solarium is another classical and charming garden room. Attached to the house it becomes a natural transition from indoors to out, bringing the garden into the living space. The solarium can be used for dining, lounging, or sleeping, as well as growing plants. After you

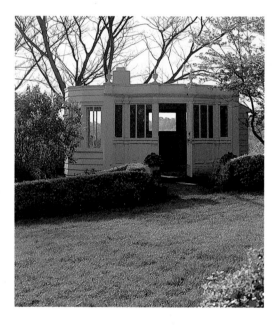

Above: This beautiful summerhouse, now in a Maryland garden, was formerly the ticket office from London's Strand Theatre. Windows at the left overlook a vista—bordered by boxwood and peonies—leading to a fountain. Right: Panels of safety glass screen a sitting area from wind and salt spray in this hillside garden overlooking the Pacific Ocean.

Left: *A path of stepping stones winds through informal flower beds to an English bench. The trellis walls in this small city garden are softened by trailing vines.* Below: *A varied plantscape provides color for a spacious seating area while also softening the bordering fence.*

have decided how the solarium will be used, you'll be able to decide more easily on the design, the importance of light exposure, and whether to locate it off a particular room (such as the dining room, living room, or bedroom). If it is to be used more for cultivating plants than as a sitting room, drainage, water, and air circulation must be carefully planned. The floor should have a drain and could be brick, tile, slate, or cement. Outdoor garden furniture is the most practical choice. If the conservatory will be used more as an additional room, with plants only as decorative touches, then upholstered furniture and even carpeting are appropriate. Solariums or conservatories are best built on solid foundations where there will be very little shifting and settling of the ground. Glass tends to crack rather than creak like wood if the structure settles.

If a deciduous tree is planted nearby, the conservatory could be used as a sunny greenhouse in winter and a cool, sitting room in summer. Glass panels can be designed with interchangeable panels of screening, which allow cool breezes and extend the conservatory or solarium's usefulness. Many prefabricated kits and frames are available from the United States, Canada, and England. Some solariums come with a roof that opens, allowing for fresh air without wind.

PERGOLAS

Pergolas were originally designed in Italy to provide shade and as a structure to grow vines and ripen grapes on. They found their way into English gardens at the turn of the twentieth century as a more permanent garden element, displaying beautiful climbing plants and providing summer shade and a covered walkway. Pergolas can be built off the house or as independent structures. Their placement is important, as it indicates direction and can encourage one to walk under them. It is important for a pergola to have a destination such as a gazebo, a seating area with a view, or a special garden. A pergola without a definite beginning or end is a path that leads nowhere—merely an arbor.

Construction can either be of lightweight wooden poles for temporary use or of solid redwood or cedar beams with columns of wood, brick, stone, stucco, or cement. Lightweight pergolas are usually more rustic, built from long, narrow trees still bearing bark. Bamboo poles can also be used and are quite beautiful with wisteria or jasmine climbing them. Narrow poles can be lashed, nailed, or notched together and should be closely placed to give a stronger sense of scale. If poles bend, place them so they arch upwards rather than sag. Lightweight pergolas are inexpensive to make and are a good temporary garden feature. They are practical for people who frequently move and for short-lived plants and smaller gardens. In a vegetable garden, gourds, melons, beans, and grapes can use a pergola for support. It provides a shaded resting spot for the gardener as well as functioning as a garden feature.

The solid pergolas give permanence, strength, and a formal quality to a garden. They can wrap around a deck or terrace, providing height, architectural interest, shade, and a frame for climbing plants. Pergolas can also be used to form transitions from the house to the garden, from one garden room to another, and even from the parking area to the front entrance.

Far left: *A vine-covered pergola serves as the transition between a wooded section of the property and an area of open lawn. This traditional Pergola (left) leads visitors along a colorful garden walk.* Above: *An arbor of wisteria offers shade and fragrance to a terrace garden. An arrangement of rock crystals creates decorative interest.*

GAZEBOS AND GARDEN HOUSES

Gazebos and garden houses add charm and distinction to the garden while providing shelter from sun, wind, and—depending on design—rain. The designs can be quite diverse—anything from a roof covering a bench to a miniature house with comfortable furniture for reading and napping. No matter how modest or elaborate, any well-designed garden house will entice visitors into the garden and be a decorative feature year round.

Many gazebos are prefabricated and can be ordered through garden magazines and catalogs. Whether you decide to assemble a mail-order one or have something custom built, placement, size, design, and use are still the major considerations after the budget. If the gazebo is close to the house, it will look better if it relates to similar architectural features or at least is constructed with the same materials. When the gazebo is not in sight of the house the range of appropriate styles is much broader. The garden house will be of sustaining interest as a garden feature even in winter when the landscape becomes more bleak. To take full advantage of the gazebo as a garden accent, place it as a focal point in the garden.

A Colonial-style

gazebo (far left) *blends in well with the*
woodland setting. Near left: *In this narrow city*
backyard, an ornate gazebo camouflages a factory wall
and also serves as a pleasant place to sit and read.
Above: *This design by Vixen Hill can be ordered*
through the mail and assembled in sections. Right: *The*
clear, simple lines of a Japanese teahouse beckon visitors
across the footbridge for a cup of hot tea on a cold
autumn day.

Courtesy of Toro Co.

Garden lights can be used to accentuate such garden and architectural features as sculpture, fountains, a gazebo, or specimen trees. They can also be used to create leaf and shadow patterns on walkways and walls, as well as to illuminate interesting foliage and paths that lead visitors through the garden.

NIGHTTIME RETREATS

A well-lit garden provides a welcome retreat for the commuter who returns home after dark seeking a place to relax. Lighting is an important design aspect; it extends the garden's useable hours, creates dramatic views, and provides safety. There are many attractive, low-voltage fixtures available. Spotlights are inexpensive and easy to install. They can be directed up into a tree to show off its shape or down the trunk to light up a walk or dining area. When illuminated, a canopy of foliage makes wonderful light patterns. Tiny canister lights can be positioned in trees for a delicate, fairyland atmosphere. Lights for illuminating pathways are available on stands of adjustable

Courtesy of Toro Co.

heights and come in designs of mushrooms, flowers, and Japanese lanterns of wood, brass, copper, or flat black or green. Footlights can be used to lead visitors into nighttime retreats in the garden. Whether the designer chooses ornamental fixtures or ones that are purely functional and recede from view in the daylight, it is important that walks be safely lit, especially near steps and tree roots. The light should not be glaring, so use frosted glass or shades to direct the light. The amount of *useable* light from a given source will vary according to the angle of the lamp and the distance from the illuminated surface. Wiring should be of exterior quality and be laid underground; all fixtures and plugs must be waterproof. In areas where insects are a problem, yellow lights will discourage them at night.

Left: *A rope hammock slung across a corner makes good use of limited space.*
Above: *This outdoor deck features a screened-in area which allows people to rest or sleep outdoors on hot nights without being pestered by insects.*

SLEEPING ARRANGEMENTS AND LOUNGING AREAS

A hammock slung under a canopy of trees is the most comfortable, inexpensive, and delightful sleeping or lounging device made for the garden. A heavy rope hammock with an oak spacing bar is designed to stay open and not enfold one like a sack of potatoes. Hammocks come in single and double widths, and if two trees with the right spacing are unavailable, a fence post secured in the ground with cement will do the trick nicely. Chaise lounges are the other most popular garden furniture for lounging. If you don't like to be off the ground or to feel a swinging motion, this is a preferable choice.

A master bedroom can be transformed into a garden room with attractive skylights. French doors might open onto a private garden balcony, deck, or terrace. An arbor might extend from the room to the outdoor space, providing another degree of privacy and creating a more intimate human scale.

On the deck or terrace a hot tub or spa can be installed for hours of delicious soaking under the stars.

A small loft could be tucked away in a secluded spot for sleeping or sunbathing—perhaps up in a tree or out a window on a flat roof with a good view—or built as an overhanging roof above the French doors. If necessary, use insect netting to make a canopy enclosure around the bed. The stars and moon will still be visible; night scents will drift by; and the excitement of the night in a hideaway spot might evoke memories and lend romance to the sleepers.

*T*his sunny deck, designed by Brickman Group, (above left) adjoins the master bedroom and is a great place for sunbathing during the summer. Above right: *A berm helps screen a sunken patio without the need for a more austere fence or wall. Edges of the flagstone patio are softened by vines, cascading shrubs, and roses.* Left: *A raised porch with sliding glass doors provides the owners of this New Jersey home with an unobstructed view of their backyard flower garden. The banana tree to the left is in a large tub that is moved indoors for the winter.*

Garden benches serve both functional and decorative needs. Above: Claude Monet's garden bench is featured in the artist's reconstructed flower garden at Giverny. Above right: The wrought-iron table at Bellingrath House (Alabama), is virtually weatherproof and indestructible. Facing page, right: An English-style teak bench features extra-wide armrests, for resting a snack tray and drinks. Facing page, far right: A swing seat strung from the strong branches of a mature tree adds a romantic touch to this small shade garden.

GARDEN SEATS AND BENCHES

Garden Seats and Benches. A seat generally accommodates one person, while benches have room for two or more. Seats and benches are usually made from wood, stone, or iron for aesthetic appeal. They can be highly formal or rustic and natural in design. For maximum comfort, seats and benches should be placed on level ground, and they may need a foundation of flagstone or gravel to prevent wobbles. With flagstone, consider planting cushions of fragrant herbs—like chamomile and thyme—between the cracks, so their spicy odor is released when trodden on. This doesn't harm the plants and indeed seems to stimulate their growth. Seats can be clustered around a table to make an inviting place for people to gather, while benches can be situated where they overlook a vista beyond the garden or a focal point within the garden.

Some classic seat and bench designs include:

Claude Monet's garden bench— sleek, wide-slatted bench, painted green, easily accommodates six people, featured in Monet's garden, Giverny, France.

Charleston Battery bench—wood slats form the back, ornate cast-iron pieces form the legs. Comfortable "park" bench popular in the historic area of Charleston, South Carolina.

Adirondack seat—high wooden back, steep seat popular in New England and the Adirondack mountains of upstate New York.

Deacon's bench—dignified, ecclesiastical design. Popular use around old homes, on porches and patios.

Sir Edward Lutyens bench—substantial ornate wood bench designed by this famous Victorian landscape architect. Makes a good focal point, particularly against a high hedge or brick wall in front of a reflecting pool.

Peacock bench—intricate wire designs evoke romantic images. Very Victorian and ephemeral in appearance.

Swing seat—usually wooden, slatted, held above the ground by chains connected to a beam, allowing the seat to swing.

Tree seat—encircles a tree, providing a view in all directions. Good for the center of a courtyard or clearing where visitors can sit anywhere on the bench and admire a pleasant view.

F acing page, below: *This ornate wrought-iron bench adds an old-fashioned look to a small city garden in Louisiana. Left: Simple benches made from wooden slabs partly encircle a vine-clad tree in a city courtyard. Below: This wooden bench follows the curve of a retaining wall that holds back soil for a flower bed. The flowing lines of the wall and bench are a good contrast to the vertical lines of the slatted fence in the background.*

chapter three

DISPLAY GARDENS

G ARDENS

have been described as "the highest form of art," because gardeners and landscape architects use plants, water, and stone to create artistic designs. However, in spite of this artistic acclaim it is unlikely that gardens will ever command the investment value of paintings or sculpture, since gardens need constant care to keep up their appearance. Neglect a painting or a sculpture by putting

Beautiful display gardens result from the combination of well-designed plantings and tasteful garden accents. Above: Without the many displays of statuary, the gardens at Versailles would lose much of their impact. Right: This sculptured wall featuring Elizabethan figures serves as a focal point at the end of an arbor. Far right, above: With a round pool and fountain as its focal point, this shade garden uses long-lasting wax begonias to edge the beds and borders and accentuate the strong circular design. The gazebo in the background leads visitors into another theme garden. Far right, below: Open areas are perfect places for water gardens featuring sun-loving water lilies. In the background, a raised bed of perennials creates a colorful border.

it in the attic, and over the years it can increase in value with no effort on the part of the owner. But neglect a garden or landscape and it soon returns to wilderness.

Nevertheless, gardens have been popular places to display investment art—particularly sculpture, although paintings, too, are often displayed in a covered garden setting in buildings that resemble "orangeries" or in elaborate summerhouses. Even the earliest known gardens were filled with naturalistic sculptures—rocks and pieces of driftwood resembling animals and birds. Indeed, the Chinese deliberately searched hillsides and ravines for interesting boulders to add to their gardens as accents, giving them names like "turtle rock" and "tiger rock" for the creatures they symbolized. In ancient Greece and Rome, gardens were favorite repositories for sculpture. Avenues were made of statues on pedestals, and special niches were created to display a bust, frieze, or figure. Statues and sculpture have become such an important feature of gardens that they are often used as focal points at the end of a vista, incorporated into fountains, or used in pairs as sentinels to announce entryways. Today, appreciation for good sculpture is so strong that some gardens have become galleries to hold and display sculpture.

Some famous sculpture gardens include *Brookgreen Gardens*, Myrtle Beach, South Carolina; *Jasmine Hill*, Montgomery, Alabama; *Cranbrook Center*, near Detroit, Michigan; the *Pepsico Sculpture Gardens*, Purchase, New York; *Toronto Sculpture Garden*, Toronto, Canada; *Nemours Garden*, Wilmington, Delaware, and the *Huntington Botanical Gardens*, San Marino, California.

Jasmine Hill is a particularly interesting sculpture garden because it is on a small scale in a woodland setting with an emphasis on marble reproductions of classical Greek sculpture. Unlike many sculpture gardens, where plants take a back seat to art for fear of overpowering the sculpture, at *Jasmine Hill* there is a very heavy em-

phasis on plants—and also water features—with the sculpture. The garden blends the sculpture and landscape so successfully that neither element suffers from an intrusion of the other. A great deal of attention is paid to "framing" the pieces—an avenue of trees forms a natural arbor and the sculpture itself is set in a clearing.

The following are some ways to display sculpture in the landscape:

- As a focal point at the end of a vista
- As a focal point at the center of a space or enclosure
- Along a wall as a gallery
- Inset into a wall or hedge—as a niche
- In pairs as sentinels to announce an entryway
- As an accent to a flower bed or mixed-shrub border
- As an accent to a water feature,

such as a pond, canal, or fountain
- Randomly placed among clearings connected by paths
- As an orderly avenue to direct an eye along a vista

The question of style is a matter of personal taste. Modernism in the garden tends to evoke controversy, since many people see abstract art as a jarring intrusion into the natural orderliness that a garden is meant to create. However, the *Pepsico Gardens* are a marvelous example of modern sculpture ingeniously placed. Scale, color, harmony, and relationship to buildings and grounds have been carefully considered as well as the creation of vistas, backgrounds, framing, and a sequence of experiences. To decide where to place a new sculpture, designer Russell Page tested different locations and various orientations with a full-scale mock-up of the sculpture. This is an excellent technique to test the scale and position of a proposed acquisition in the home landscape, as well as to determine the height and shape of the required base before actually placing a heavy piece of sculpture.

With the passing of time, even machines can become desirable garden ornamentals. Old ploughs, cogwheels, winches, capstans, wagon wheels, and other industrial artifacts have found their way into gardens as ornamentation.

Just as a collection of artwork can be displayed in a landscape, so can plants be used as "collections" to create interesting theme gardens. Collections of a particular plant family or genus—such as ferns, rhododendrons, grasses, or roses—can be planted creatively so they are more than a botanical collection. In addition, plants can be grouped according to a common feature. A collection of alpines can be made into a rock garden, annuals used to make a courtyard garden, perennials to represent an English Cottage garden, spring-flowering bulbs to make a Dutch garden, and aquatics to create an imaginative water garden.

Also, plants can be used to make theme gardens of a single color or group of colors. An all white garden, a blue and white garden, or a white, silver, and grey garden are examples of effective color themes. In addition to flowering plants, it's important to introduce plants with foliage colors that match the required theme. For example, "grey gardens" are popular at the seashore, since a large number of plants with grey foliage—sea cotton, grazanias, Russian-olive, and dusty millers—will tolerate salt conditions.

Consider the quality of natural light in your garden environment. The light strongly affects color; pale colors look best in soft, misty light and look washed out and faded in strong, bright light. Hot colors look good in sunny Mediterranean climates. Purple-blue glows at twilight, and white reflects the moon's light and will also brighten a shady corner and subdue a bright color scheme.

PLANT GROUP GARDENS:

Following are some display gardens that use groups of plants, with brief comments on how each works well in the landscape.

ANNUAL FLOWER GARDEN:

Annuals are plants that complete their life cycles in a single season—germinating from seed, flowering, setting seed, and dying. Since their life cycles are short, their flowering displays are the most spectacular of all plants. Some annuals stay in bloom all season, producing a continuous flowering display of ten weeks or more.

Annuals offer the opportunity to create "instant color" for containers, window boxes, beds, and borders. Because of their immense range of colors and shapes and their various growing requirements, annuals can put on a three-to-six-month display anywhere in the garden. Color schemes can be easily changed and even coordinated to the interior decoration of the home.

Annuals are often used for "carpet bedding," to informally edge a lawn or in formal garden beds of geometric shapes. They are frequently mixed in with perennials to bolster the relatively short flowering display of many perennials. Annuals are the predominant flower group used in "cutting gardens," where plants must have long stems and the ability to recover from constant cutting. The use of annuals is economical and time-saving. Some seeds can be sowed directly in the ground without transplanting. Seeds offer a far greater variety than pre-grown plants.

Beds and borders composed primarily of flowering annuals (above left) *welcome visitors to this otherwise austere entrance.* Left: *Triploid hybrid marigolds create a golden color throughout the summer in this small, secret garden with a Japanese touch.*

This perennial garden on Long Island is sheltered from wind and salt spray by a guest cottage (left), barn, and tool shed. Below left: Yellow-flowered and dark red tree peonies provide perennial color along a gravel path, flowering at the same time as the golden chaintree in the background.

Below: Flowering azaleas, evergreen shrubs, and low-growing perennials—especially moss pinks—create a beautiful foundation planting around a suburban home.

PERENNIAL FLOWER GARDEN:

Perennials usually produce foliage growth the first year and flower the second year, continuing to flower each year thereafter. The flowering period of most perennials is about three weeks, and so many perennial gardens are planted to reach peak color at a particular time of year—usually mid-June or early July in most of the United States and Canada. The most effective perennial plantings require very careful selection, placement, blending of color, textures, and forms of plants. If consideration is given to foliage, berries, and seed pods, as well as flower color, the border will be attractive for long periods of time. Gertrude Jekyll, the turn-of-the-century English painter and embroiderer-turned-gardener, is still considered the foremost authority of designing perennial beds with a tapestry effect. She perfected the double perennial border, whereby parallel beds of perennials are planted against a tall, dark-green hedge or stone wall, the beds separated by a path. A statue or gazebo is often located at the end of the path as a focal point.

FLOWERING BULB GARDEN:

For the most part, flowering bulbs are divided into spring-flowering and summer-flowering categories. Tulips and daffodils are the most popular spring-flowering bulbs, while dahlias and gladioli are the most popular summer-flowering bulbs. Tulips offer an incredibly wide color range and are excellent for formal beds and borders—most often in places where annuals will be used later in the season to provide summer color. Daffodils look best planted informally in drifts at the edge of a lawn, clustered under trees, as mass plantings along a stream bank, or beside a pond. A special group of early flowering bulbs are important for "winter gardens," since they will frequently bloom before the last winter snowfall. These include aconites, snowdrops, snow crocuses, *Iris reticulata,* and *Anemone blanda.* Many bulbs have the advantage of "naturalizing"—they will multiply, and continue to come up year after year without replanting—a great advantage for informal plantings. Keep this in mind when planting, and give the bulbs extra bonemeal and compost for heartier plants and healthier blooms.

HERB GARDEN:

A relatively small number of herbs have ornamental flowers. More often, they have interesting foliage colors, fragrances, and textures. They are grown mostly for culinary, medicinal, and cosmetic value and require particularly careful planting to create an appealing display. A popular layout for an herb garden is a cartwheel design in which paths radiate from the center like the spokes of a wheel, with herbs placed in beds between the spokes. Usually a bee-hive, sundial, or birdbath is placed at the center as an accent. Herbs can also be planted to make intricate "knot gardens," choosing dwarf kinds of various colored foliages that are trimmed to create low hedges. Sometimes the spaces between the hedges are filled in with colored gravel so when seen from above, the appearance is that of a stained-glass window.

ORNAMENTAL GRASS GARDEN:

Ornamental grasses are best displayed as a border—sometimes edging a lake, pond, or pool—with tall varieties situated so as not to obscure the lower growing kinds. Since bamboo is a genus of grass, a collection of bamboo also complements grass gardens. Ornamental grasses are excellent for planting around swimming pools, since they require little maintenance and do not attract bees like other plants. Grasses provide wonderful textures and accents to perennial borders and make excellent ground covers. Many ornamental grasses are drought tolerant, require no mowing, and are deer resistant. Colors vary from silver to blue and gold to red shades.

POPULAR ORNAMENTAL GRASSES

Pampas grass *(Cortadera selloana)*
Fountain grass *(Pennisetum alopecuroides* white flowers and *P. setaceum* pink flowers)
Blue fescue *(Festuca ovina glauca)*
Ribbon grass *(Phalaris arundinacea picta)*
Feather grass *(Stipa gigantea)*
Zebra grass *(Miscanthus sinensis 'Zebrinus')*

Designed by landscape architects, Oehme, van Sweden and Associates, Inc.

Although gardens accented with ornamental grasses have long been popular in Europe, it has been the landscape architecture firm, Oehme, van Sweden and Associates, Inc. that has introduced garden designs with ornamental grasses to the United States. This page and the top far right illustrate some of the variety of colors, textures, and movement grasses offer.

Designed by landscape architects, Oehme, van Sweden and Associates, Inc.

AQUATIC PLANTS— WATER GARDEN:

Water lilies, lotus, water poppies, water lettuce, papyrus, duckweed, cattails, flag iris, and arrowhead are all examples of plants that grow and flower with their roots permanently immersed in water. They can be displayed in formal or free-form pools, ponds, lakes, and even streams where the flow is slowed by a dam. Generally speaking, in formal pools the use of water plants is subdued, since the purpose of formal pools is usually to complement the architectural lines of a nearby building or to reflect some attractive nearby feature. However, informal pools and ponds can be more densely planted with waterside foliage plants of grasses and sedges, ferns, reeds and rushes, and the large round leaves of *Petasites japonicus, Gunnera manicata*, and *Hostas*. Good tree choices include the Japanese maples *(Acer griseum, A. japonicum, A. negundo,* and *A. palmatum),* weeping willows (*Salix X chrysocoma*), cut-leaved alder, birch, and swamp cypress. Appropriate shrubs include azaleas, rhododendrons, and hydrangeas. Astilbe, Iris (*I. japonica, I. sibirica, I. Kaempferi*), primroses, daylilies, and *Agapanthus* all make lovely flowering border plants.

Designed by landscape architects, Oehme, van Sweden and Associates, Inc.

Designed by landscape architects, Oehme, van Sweden and Associates, Inc.

*T*he formal lines of this elegant water garden (above) are contrasted with the soft informal plant shapes; designed for Mr. and Mrs. Vollmer by landscape architects, Oehme, van Sweden and Associates, Inc. Boulders and river stone (right) create a naturalistic setting for this waterlily pool. Water-loving plants demand their own unique culture; placed next to regal Japanese iris, waterlilies grown in underwater tubs are reminiscent of Monet.

WILDFLOWERS— MEADOW AND WOODLAND GARDENS:

Planting wildflowers adds delicate beauty and intrigue to a cultivated garden and also helps to preserve some of the rare and endangered plant varieties. In dry climates, plant seed in the autumn before the winter rains. Where winters are severe, time plantings so they are established before freezing temperatures. The notion that you can scatter wildflower seed like chicken feed across a meadow and expect a riot of color among the native weeds and grasses is quite mistaken. Either plough the meadow first to ensure that the wildflower seed comes into contact with fertile, bare soil, free of grass and weed competition, or else dig up island beds among the meadow grass to have drifts of wildflowers. In addition to meadow plantings, wildflowers can be used in woodland, since special kinds will tolerate light shade. Since most woodland wildflowers sprout, flower, and set seeds even before deciduous trees are in full leaf, it is wisest to choose plants that bloom in early spring for a woodland garden.

Facing page: Wildflowers provide a great variety of vivid colors, patterns, and shapes. After the initial soil preparation and seeding, very little maintenance is required for natural planting. Choose seed mixtures that are native to your area so they can readily re-seed and establish themselves. Wildflowers should be cultivated informally in natural drifts.

ALPINE GARDEN:

A rock garden is the best place to display alpines. Most alpines are diminutive plants that don't produce a lavish floral display, so they can be planted in quite small spaces, including stone troughs and dry walls. A collection of stone troughs on a patio or decorating a courtyard is an attractive landscape accent. Sedums are an important group to consider for long-lasting color. Many have red, blue, and silvery succulent leaves in beautiful star shapes and egg-shaped clusters.

True alpine gardens require specific, fast-draining conditions such as rocky soils and cool climates, and a dedicated, knowledgeable gardener. The results give a charming effect much like a miniature alpine meadow. Many rock-garden plants are perfect between stepping-stones and along the risers of stone steps. Like native plants and wildflowers, rock-garden plants look best without competition from showy ornamentals.

SINGLE GENUS GARDENS

Because certain families of plants are so striking and offer such a wide range of colors and heights, it's worth considering the design of a garden space devoted almost entirely to a single family.

AZALEA GARDEN:

Since azaleas are a class of rhododendron, usually displaying smaller flowers and smaller leaves, both azaleas and rhododendrons can be interplanted. They work especially well planted on a wooded lot, where tall trees provide light shade, or used in drifts on acid soil with paths wandering through the mass plantings. In addition to early, mid-season, and late cultivars, consider native North American species and "deciduous" azaleas (such as the Exbury types), many of which are heavily fragrant.

BOXWOOD GARDEN:

When left unpruned, these slow-growing evergreen shrubs make billowing mounds and form private garden spaces. Also, plants can be trimmed severely to make a clean, sharp outline for formal designs—indispensable for parterre gardens, where beds and borders are edged with low hedges. Boxwood is popular in Southern gardens because it has a cooling effect when planted around flagstone and lawn. The branches must be kept clear of snow to avoid browning the leaves.

CAMELLIA GARDEN:

Camellias are well-suited to mid-climate areas, because their blooming period is extensive if both the *C. sasanqua* (fall flowering) and *C. japonica* (early spring flowering) varieties are used. Collections work well when displayed in a woodland setting where high trees provide light shade, or

Azaleas planted in masses (left) create a colorful impact in a garden. Below: Boxwood gardens provide a cool, green environment during hot summers, and clearly defined shape when the earth is covered in snow. Facing page, right: Irises planted in masses of rich color provide a spectacular theme for any garden. Far right: Roses are a favorite for theme gardens because they provide such a variety of color, scent, and growth habits, while invoking a romantic atmosphere.

when planted as avenues to form "tunnels" along a path (the path becomes covered with spent petals, like confetti). On a smaller scale, camellias can be used in formal gardens, espaliered against walls, and displayed in decorative containers.

FERN GARDEN:

Excellent for moist, shady places or when used informally with boulders and waterfalls as accents, ferns also work well around ruins, grottoes, and along stream banks. Growing tree ferns in tubs makes it easy to move them indoors during freezing weather.

IRIS GARDEN:

With the exception of tulips, no genus has as rich a color range as iris, pariculary the bearded iris. Though their flowering display is confined to several weeks during late spring or early summer, flag iris, Japanese iris, and Siberian iris can be used effectively to prolong the display. Bearded iris is sensational planted either in mixtures as a "rainbow border" or informally as clumps of separate colors along the edge of a stream.

LILAC GARDEN:

Lilacs are usually planted in combination with other heavily fragrant plants, such as roses, to create a "fragrance garden." A simple design for a lilac garden is a semicircle flanking a bench, gazebo, or summerhouse, with an area of flagstone where fragrant herbs—especially chamomile and thyme—can be planted in the cracks. The floral display from lilacs is not long-lasting, so not much garden space should be devoted to them. However, a quiet nook in a corner is an ideal place for this romantic theme garden.

ROSE GARDEN:

Probably more popular than any other genus, roses make an especially good theme garden because the blooming period is extensive, and a wide range of plant habits enables designers to use roses in a number of appealing ways. Dwarf varieties create masses of horizontal color when used for bedding, while climbing varieties, if trained up arbors, trellises, and pergolas, extend color high into the sky. Tree-form roses can be used in containers and dwarf hedging roses as edging to flower borders.

ADDITIONAL SINGLE GENUS THEME GARDENS

Bamboo Garden	Hosta Garden
Cactus Garden	Marigold Garden
Daylily Garden	Orchid Garden
Fuschia Garden	Palm Garden
Hibiscus Garden	Peony Garden

SINGLE COLOR GARDENS

Though many people want to see a rainbow of color in the landscape, a section of garden planted all in one color can also be appealing. Single-color gardens are sometimes quite temporary and designed to commemorate a special occasion. For example, an all-white garden might be planted one year for the specific purpose of providing a romantic aura for a forthcoming wedding. The next season, for the sake of a golden wedding anniversary, the same space might be planted with an all-gold theme, using yellow, orange, and golden-colored flowers.

Following are some single-color gardens that are quite easy to create, with examples of the plants that might go in them.

WHITE GARDEN:

White roses, gladiolus, candytuft, feverfew, baby's breath, white pansies, clematis, madonna lilies, white petunias, marguerites, shasta daisies, cala lilies, white cosmos, wisteria, lilac, azaleas, phlox, hydrangea primula obconica, geraniums, foxglove, tulips, cyclamen, agapanthus, alyssum, as well as shrubs with cream or white variegated foliage and trees with white blossoms, like dogwood.

RED GARDEN:

Zinnias, petunias, poppies, cardinal flower, red honeysuckle, red clematis, red dahlias, red gladiolus, oriental poppies, begonias, impatiens, red coleus, red salvia, red roses, and red tulips.

GREY OR SILVER GARDEN:

Dusty millers, santolina, gypsophila, anaphalis, chamomile, lamb's ears, artemisias, cardoon, Scotch thistle, daily bush (*Olearia*), lavender, catmint (*nepeta*), yarrow (Achillea X moonshine), aubrieta, artichokes, and yuccas.

BLUE GARDEN:

Wisteria, cornflowers, blue lace flower, nemophila, lilac, iris, morning-glories, forget-me-nots, ageratum, delphinium, blue petunias, rosemary, cineraria, blue pansies and violas, felicia, blue fuscue, lobelia, blue salvia, companula, ceanothus, lupins, crainsbill geraniums, blue agapanthus, vinca, blue primroses, and asters.

A grey and white theme predominates in this perennial garden, with just a touch of blue and pink from roses and irises.

In this garden in the Ladew Topiary Gardens in Maryland (above), the yellow theme is produced not only from yellow flowers such as tulips, but also from shrubs with yellow leaves. The Oriental style gazebo echoes the yellow theme of the garden. This green garden in Princeton, New Jersey (above right) features evergreens, including English boxwood and ivy, and a spiky-leafed yucca. The preponderance of greens has a cool, soothing effect.

PINK GARDEN:

Pink petunias, pink geraniums, pink snapdragons, azaleas, cosmos, cleome, pink chrysanthemums, pink dianthus, pink gladiolus, pink roses like "Queen Elizabeth," hollyhocks, impatiens, primroses, tulips, pink camellias, and rhododendrons.

GREEN GARDEN:

Boxwood, helleborus, green gladiolus, green zinnias, green nicotiana, as well as many kinds of shrubs with distinctive green foliage—from the black-green of certain hollies to the lime-green of varieties of enonymus.

YELLOW OR GOLD GARDENS:

Marigolds, coreopsis, yellow iris, deciduous azaleas, yellow privet, yellow barberry, laburnum, kerria, Scotch broom, chrysanthemums, golden juniper, basket of gold, sunflowers, nasturtiums, rudbeckia, helianthus, evening primroses, calendulas, day lilies, and yellow roses.

THEME GARDENS

The history of ornamental gardens extends from the ancient Egyptian and Chinese civilizations over a period of more than two thousand years to the present day. Styles of garden design have changed from generation to generation and from country to country, from the grandiose Italian and French Renaissance gardens to the more intimate Japanese meditation gardens and the English cottage gardens. Following is a list of popular garden styles named for the period or country of origin, with some comments on the main elements that distinguish each garden style.

AMERICAN COLONIAL GARDEN:

Characterized by white picket fences, boxwood parterres, brick paths, holly clipped into cone shapes, seats recessed into alcoves, covered wells, ornamental outhouses, pleached *allées*, hollyhocks, sweet peas, and cottage pinks that helped Colonial families remember gardens in Europe.

BIBLICAL GARDEN:

Usually laid out in the shape of a cross, embellished with statues representing biblical figures—especially reproductions of Michaelangelo's *David*, the Madonna, Adam and Eve. Plants generally include figs, olive trees, lilies, and palms; other accents include seats and fountains with ecclesiastical motifs.

CHINESE GARDEN:

A heavy emphasis on dramatic rocks, trickling water, and shrubs pruned into bizarre shapes. Plants include camellias, rhododendrons, and azaleas. Structures are predominently shelters and viewing platforms of bamboo construction; also "moongates," winding gravel trails, statuary featuring dragons, and other mythical figures.

*C*olonial gardens (left) *are a most appropriate accent to a Colonial-style house. The use of boxwood, a small white garden shed, and a picket fence are essential elements. Colonial Williamsburg in Virginia, has preserved many outstanding examples of Colonial gardens.* Below right: *A biblical garden usually includes plants mentioned in the Bible, many of which contain medicinal herbs.* Above right: *"Orderly disorder" describes a typical English cottage garden abundant with mixtures of roses, perennials, bulbs, and annuals. The flower beds spill into pathways and stray right up to the front door.*

DUTCH GARDEN:

Generally features a windmill or draw-bridge as a focal point, surrounded by beds of tulips, daffodils, and other spring-flowering bulbs, which are followed by colorful annuals and perennials, particularly from former Dutch possessions such as South Africa. Heavy summer emphasis on gladioli, dahlias, and garden lilies; plastered walls, delft tiles, and birdboxes that reflect Dutch architecture.

EGYPTIAN GARDEN:

Formal layout, usually with a canal or rectangular reflecting pool as the central feature. Citrus, fig, and myrtle trees in containers. Papyrus, lotus, and date palms.

ENGLISH COTTAGE GARDEN:

Emphasis on flowering plants, particularly annuals and perennials, densely planted. Strong sense of informality. Usually a dry wall brimming with succulents and alpine plants, lots of climbing roses, a rustic seat, birdbath or birdhouse accents, manicured free-form lawn, and flagstone paths.

FRENCH RENAISSANCE GARDEN:

Long, wide vistas. Avenues of statuary and/or topiary evergreens. Elaborate parterre gardens filled with bedding plants. Baroque fountains, expansive reflecting pools, trelliswork. Temples, orangeries, and long terraces.

GREEK GARDEN:

Statuary representing figures from Greek mythology. Busts on pedestals, columns, urns, formal reflecting pools decorated with scenes from Greek tragedy and battles. Trees in tubs.

INDIAN GARDEN:

Geometrical layout—mostly squares and rectangles, lots of reflecting pools, canals, moats, and fountains with voluptuous maidens. Statuary in the form of elephants, Indian gods, cobras, and tigers. Crepe myrtles, lotus, marigolds, coleus, and cannas; fig trees with roots snaking over steps and stone slabs. Lots of gold embellishment.

ITALIAN RENAISSANCE GARDEN:

Steep hillsides with steps, terraces, and gushing fountains. Long vistas. Boxwood parterres, grottoes, walls with tiles, and mosaics. Geranimums, calla lilies, tall cypress trees, citrus in urns, pergolas, topiary evergreens. Strong architectural features.

JAPANESE GARDEN:

Strong sense of symbolism and serenity, using mostly water, natural stones, and shrubs. Three quarters of plants are generally evergreen. Clumps of bamboo, azaleas pruned into mounds, and camellias with exposed, sinuous trunks are strongly represented. Also wisteria, ornamental cherries, waterlilies, and Japanese iris. Stone towers, pagodas, and lanterns are familiar accents, as well as winding gravel paths, cobblestones, and zig-zag bridges.

MEDIEVAL GARDEN:

Usually walled in brick or stone with a heavy oak Gothic doorway as an entrance. Ruined arch frequently located in the middle as an accent. Emphasis on strict formal-

Above, left: *The Italian Renaissance theme is best reserved for large, formal gardens with grand scale proportions. Above: Japanese gardens are much more adaptable and can be tucked into a small courtyard or interwoven in a stone or pebbled pathway. Facing page: A Southern garden may include a natural swamp and over-grown flowering vines clinging to the trees, or it could be well manicured with boxwood and azaleas.*

bed I lie,'' for example. A statue of Shakespeare usually forms an accent in the garden, and other Shakespearean characters may be represented in sculpture. Since Shakespeare lived in the Elizabethan era, the design is usually Elizabethan in style, with brickwork, benches, and arbors.

SOUTHERN GARDEN:

Wisteria trained over arbors, banksia and Cherokee roses scrambling up walls and fences, indica azaleas, camellias, evergreen grandiflora magnolias and yaupon holly trimmed into cones are hallmarks of a Southern-style garden. Usually, there is a flagstone patio rimmed with boxwood and shaded with a live oak, wrought iron furniture, or a Charleston battery bench (wooden slats and iron end pieces), and a cool formal fountain with a pair of herons or a cherub scuplture. Huge grandiflora roses, calla lilies, caladiums, and crepe myrtles are also hallmarks of a Southern-style garden.

SPANISH GARDEN:

Usually an enclosure formed completely by archways or by a wall of arches with a hexagonal well or fountain set in the middle and sleek channels of water radiating out to the edges which irrigate formal beds planted mostly with annuals. Lots of tilework, decorated urns, and flowering vines (especially bougainvillea). Popular style for other mild-climate areas.

ity of design (sometimes ecclesiastical) but an informality of plantings, beds, and borders brimming with pinks, lavender, violas, roses, flowering bulbs, and herbs—especially medicinal herbs.

PERSIAN GARDEN:

Shares many similarities with Indian and Spanish gardens because of the Moslem Empire, which stretched from Spain to India. Persian gardens are usually walled, with a pavillion as a strong, structural accent. A network of ''runnels'' (narrow water channels) is usually laid out like a grid with a fountain at the main intersections. Sculpture and statues are absent because these images were forbidden by the Koran, but birds and fragrant flowers are important features. Plums and apricots are valued for

their flowers and fruit. Tulips, lilacs, lilies, and roses are favorite ornamental plants.

ROMAN GARDEN:

Mostly courtyard gardens, highly formal with columns, statues, reflecting pools, urns, and balustrades. Lots of geometric shapes, clipped boxwood hedges, topiary figures. Romans also loved roses, seats, and gushing water.

SHAKESPEARE GARDEN:

Simply a garden designed with plants referred to in the works of William Shakespeare. Generally formal, with tablets quoting a particular reference—''In a cowslip's

VICTORIAN GARDEN:

A white gazebo with a pineapple on top, a sleek, trellised footbridge traversing a stream, a quaint summerhouse with lots of ''gingerbread'' trim, latticework arbors, ornate pergolas, a game of croquet on the lawn, ferns mingling with hollyhocks, serpentine, single-color flower beds, tubs of exotic plants such as a container-grown banana, an Hawaiian tree fern, or a billow-

ing angel's trumpet, lots of flowering vines like clematis, jasmine, and morning-glories, nasturtiums in hanging baskets, geraniums and vinca cascading from massive urns—all these extravagant touches typify a Victorian garden.

Following are examples of theme gardens not based on a period or country.

BUTTERFLY GARDEN:

Deliberately planted to attract butterflies. Masses of flowering plants, especially marigolds, zinnias, buddleia, lythrum, and butterfly weed. Butterfly gardens generally feature a butterfly sculpture or a mosaic to emphasize the butterfly theme.

FOLLY GARDEN:

Follies are usually buildings that combine extravagance with a hint of foolishness. Follies most often are deliberately made ruins or massive wooden structures that help to decorate the horizon—pseudo temples and pavillions. Follies are often decorated with vines and surrounded by whimsical or bizarre sculpture.

FRAGRANCE GARDEN:

Abundantly planted with highly fragrant plants, particularly those that do not need to be crushed or bruised to release their aroma—such as scented-leaf geraniums, gardenias, wisteria, hyacinth, jasmine, pittosporum, and honeysuckle.

HUMMINGBIRD GARDEN:

Like butterflies, hummingbirds are attracted to certain plants—especially those colored red or orange. They are particularly fond of trumpet vines, seeking nectar with their curved beaks. Petunias, nasturtiums, penstemon, monarda, and fuchsias are also appealing to hummingbirds. As an additional attraction, hang hummingbird feeders so they can be observed from a porch or picture window.

MAZE GARDEN:

Features a labyrinth, usually grown from holly, hemlock, or boxwood. The most popular design is the maze at Hampton Court, England—reportedly the world's oldest hedge maze. Mazes don't have to be made of hedges, they can be patterns on the ground made from herbs, gravel, or tiles.

MOON GARDEN:

A garden specifically intended to be admired by moonlight, usually with a heavy concentration of plants with pale foliage and white flowers, or flowers that release their perfume at night—like night-scented stocks.

ORCHARD GARDEN:

By planting dwarf fruit trees in tubs, it's possible to have an "orchard" of fruit trees in a small area. Also, many fruit trees (including apples, pears, peaches, and plums) can be trained along a wall or fence as espaliers. Where space permits, a planting of standard-size trees can be enhanced by interplanting ornamental varieties of crabapples, peaches, pears, and plums, which will aid in the pollination of the fruit-bearing cultivars. Orchard trees can also be under-planted with flowering bulbs, such as daffodils, and meadow wildflowers (especially cowslips, cornflowers, poppies, and ox-eye daisies). A rustic bench and table provide a delightful place for picnics, and the area can be enclosed with appropriate fencing, such as sheep hurdles.

SUNDIAL GARDEN:

Features a sundial as an accent. The sundial itself can either be on a pedestal, with a stone or metal face, or else laid flat on the ground. Flat sundials frequently occupy a considerable area—even large enough to walk over. Usually sundial gardens are formal in design and in small, intimate places.

TOPIARY GARDEN:

Collection of shrubs sheared into whimsical shapes, usually of boxwood or yew. Wire forms are also created to train creeping fig (*Ficus pumila*) or needlepoint ivy over the frame. Plant flowering plants, such as wax begonias, impatiens, or sedums, into the wire structures, which are lined with moss and filled with soil. The result is very colorful. Animals and chess pieces are particularly popular shapes.

WINTER GARDEN:

Since most of North America is subject to snow cover in winter and wintry weather can last for almost six months, it makes sense to plant a garden area that will look attractive between the first frost of autumn and the last frost of spring. Do this with berry bushes, trees, and shrubs with colorful bark (red-twig maple and paper-bark cherries, for example), plus early flowering bulbs like snowdrops, aconites, and snow crocus. Ornamental grasses also work well in a winter garden, since many varieties change color and texture during the cold months.

MISCELLANEOUS THEME GARDENS:

The number of theme gardens is limited only by one's imagination. There is a garden at Sezincote in England, known as the Snake Garden. It is a sunken garden, cold and dark, with a massive metal python coiled around a column. The python rises from a pool filled with aquatic plants, and a recirculating pump spurts water from the python's mouth.

At Ladew Topiary Gardens, near Baltimore, Maryland, there is a Keyhole Garden—a circular garden room entered through a gap in the hedge shaped like a keyhole. In total, twenty other "theme" gardens are displayed on the property.

F*acing page, top: The temple for Venus, the Goddess of Love, was placed so it would reflect in the water channel. Facing page, bottom: Boxwood is a popular shrub for mazes because it grows densely and lasts for hundreds of years. Because it grows only one inch per year, the enormous task of pruning is curtailed. Left: Gardens with berries, evergreen foliage, and interesting bark textures look beautiful throughout the winter. Above: Topiary is sculpting plants, requiring patience, creative pruning, and training.*

FRAMING A VIEW

H. Thomas Hallowell Jr., owner-designer of the 50-acre Deerfield Garden near Philadelphia, says he doesn't like to turn his head more than twenty degrees without seeing a pretty picture. His English-style garden, which includes scenes reminiscent of an English deer park and English woodland gardens, is famous for its spectacular vistas. The vistas not only have distant objects as focal points, but also use definite vantage points—a gap in a hedge or a clearing among trees—to "frame" the view, just like a frame for a painting. Focal points may be structures such as a springhouse nestled in the cleft of a slope, a footbridge crossing a spillway of a pond, or a maze made from boxwood hedges, or they may be particularly beautiful specimen trees, such as a weeping Norway spruce, a clump of white birch, or a Japanese maple.

Other devices that successfully frame a view—especially in small gardens—include evergreen archways, stone moongates, vine-covered pergolas, pairs of trees planted as sentinels, marble columns, brick pillars, and rose-covered arbors made from trelliswork. Windows in fences and walls can be strategically located to frame a view.

*F*raming a view can be done with structures such as fences, keyholes in walls and gates, or with trees and shrubs pruned to form arches. A camera view finder is an excellent way to discover a vista that could be opened up, or a pattern or shape that could be repeated. If a spectacular, natural view doesn't exist, a garden feature can be framed to form an attractive view. Bulbs, such as tulips, are most effective when massed together in one color, or in a complimentary blend planted to bloom all at once. The result is spectacular and, in cool climates, can last two to three weeks. To camouflage spent bulb foliage (which must remain to nourish the bulbs for the next year), use a cover planting of annuals such as pansies, violas, nemisia, alyssum, or lobelia.

chapter four

WELCOMING AREAS

M<small>ANY</small>
homes have two entrances: the entrance to the property itself and the entrance to the house. The design of each should be considered separately. For example, an owner may want the entrance to his property to be understated or even hidden for reasons of privacy and security. A high hedge or strong gate may be desirable to discourage trespassers. But beyond the boundaries of the property, the approach to the house can say "welcome" in many ways.

FRONT ENTRANCES

The first step to welcoming visitors is to get them to the right house! Make sure the address is clearly visible from the street and illuminated at night. Well-defined and easily negotiated pathways should lead to the desired entrance. The walkway to the front door should be wide enough for a couple to walk together. It is most frustrating to wander through shrubs and trash cans searching for the front door because the entrance is unclearly marked. Eliminate all overhanging tree branches, odd steps, cracked pavement, and overgrown ground cover that wait to trip a pedestrian.

The entrance is the first impression given to visitors. Passing through a special gate, walking into an entrance courtyard, or under an arbor-lined walkway provides guests with a feeling of arrival and fills them with anticipation for the hospitality yet to come.

Most landscape design is concerned with what is seen, but consider stimulating the other senses as well. The welcoming scent of flowers, the relaxing sound of water, and the feel of a smooth brass door-knob or polished banister will add pleasant and lasting impressions.

At the front door landing allow enough room for at least three or four people to stand comfortably while waiting for the door to be answered or when saying good-bye. Also, allow ample space for the outward swing of a screen door to prevent guests from being swept away. Plan space for potted plants to enable the use of seasonal color without crowding. Container plants arranged at various heights and in specific color groups and styles will set the tone for any occasion. The effect of a formal entry can be achieved by paired standards, topiary, espaliered shrubs, or the use of only one or two colors, such as blue and white. In a cool shaded entry, add scarlet impatiens or hot pink azaleas to warm up the arrival. A solid front door painted a cheery red, an elegant hunter's green, or stained in a natural finish and given the extra touch of a brass knocker, a wreath, or a basket of flowers all say "Welcome; we are expecting you!"

An overhanging roof protects visitors and specimen plants from the weather. If wind at the door is a concern, a screen can solve the problem. Window glass can be installed with the same materials the house uses, and will allow light without blocking the view. Proportioning the landing to the house will determine its overall style and scale.

Facing page: *A red door flanked with flowers and distinctively lit with lanterns is always inviting.* Above left: *A handsome yet easily negotiated walk, and the bench, welcome the visitor to the front door. An overhanging roof covered with flowers* (above right) *tells visitors to expect a relaxing visit. The front door* (below right), *framed with an arbor of English ivy, is reminiscent of a fairy-tale cottage. The wide stoop will comfortably accommodate several visitors.*

WALKWAYS

Walkways may either be designed to get you where you're going quickly and efficiently or to help slow you down so you can enjoy the experience. Curved walkways are graceful; they slow one down to a stroll and can be used to create surprises, as not all the garden can be seen at once. Curves initially can be laid out with garden hoses. They are easily adjusted, stay in place, and illustrate many shapes and patterns. If the walk is intended for heavy traffic or the carrying of packages (from groceries to furniture), straight walks are more practical.

Straight walks give a more formal, linear look to a landscape. If flower borders lining the walkway are intended to spill over the edges, it usually looks best to begin with straight lines. A good example is Monet's garden in Giverny. In winter and early spring the garden is a crisp gridwork of straight paths. By midsummer the nasturtiums have spilled over the Grande Allée; aubrieta, dianthus, and lavender have billowed and erased all trace of the straight garden lanes. The tried and true method of using stakes and tightly-drawn string is still the best way to lay out straight lines. Measure two feet (61 centimeters) of width for each person to walk down the path. Keep in mind the proportions of the house and entrance size, as well as the traffic the walk will have and the growth habits of bordering plants.

Main walkways should be pitched for good drainage; ⅛-inch (3 millimeters) cross-slope for every one foot (30 centimeters) width of walkway will provide for water runoff and not be noticeable when walking. Four feet (1.2 meters) is the minimum width for a couple walking abreast with room for a little overhang from edging plants. A main walk five to six feet (1.5 to 1.8 meters) wide adds grace and comfort. A larger estate, of course, calls for a grander width than a small cottage.

At Versailles, Le Nortre skillfully proportioned the landscape with vistas, walkways, and steps to create the impression that

F acing page: *Curved walks
provide a leisurely introduction to a garden. Straight
walkways* (above and right) *are more formal, and
require less negotiation than curved paths. When
accented with topiary, the eye is interrupted and the
walk appears longer than it is.*

Left: *A broken flagstone path curves around a perennial garden, leading to the back gate. The stones can be interplanted with fragrant herbs and are less formal than uniformly cut stone. A focal point such as a fountain at the end of a walk, provides a year-round focus even when covered with autumn leaves.*

Louis XIV was the sun king, the center of his universe. In design there is a ratio called the "golden mean rectangle." Simplified, it refers to a proportion of 10 feet (3 meters) of width to 16 feet (4.9 meters) of length. This is a helpful ratio to work with when designing rectangular spaces, such as terraces, decks, and lawns.

Surfaces of walkways are as important a consideration as the design itself. The surface material makes a substantial difference in construction costs, long-term maintenance requirements, functional aspects, and the overall design effect the path gives to the landscape.

There are three main categories of walkway materials: soft, variable, and hard surfaces. Soft surfaces include crushed rock, packed earth, lawn turf, river rock, and wood chips. These surfaces are relatively inexpensive to install but have high maintenance requirements. They are susceptible to erosion and can only take light traffic. Soft materials blend easily and are suitable for less-traveled, narrow garden paths.

Variable surfaces include cobblestone, exposed aggregate, flagstone, sand-laid brick, wood decking, and redwood rounds in sand. These surfaces require moderate maintenance and have medium-to-high installation costs. They are traditional and beautiful and add charm to the landscape. The wide joints between the material can catch heels, narrow wheels (baby strollers, bicycles, wheelchairs), and canes and make walking difficult. Joints should be no wider than one half inch (1.2 centimeters) and filled to help prevent accidents. Ice and snow can be difficult to remove and

A mosaic pattern like the one below can be achieved with geometrically placed stones. A walkway like this one will dominate the garden design. Right: Brick is a favorite material due to its versatility, ability to blend into any setting, and its availability.

may damage the surface. Wooden treads can be slippery when wet and dangerous if poorly spaced. These safety considerations are important to keep in mind, especially when selecting surfaces for front walks and paths used frequently at night.

The third category, hard surfaces, are the most expensive to install but have the lowest maintenance costs. They include asphalt, concrete, and tile or brick laid in concrete. Such pavings provide a more formal walk with firm and regular surfaces. It is easy to remove ice and snow without

damage to the surface. Hard surfaces are preferable where heavy traffic is expected and minimum maintenance is desired. Elderly and disabled people can move more easily on firm, smooth surfaces.

There are many attractive ways to work with concrete. It is so versatile that virtually any color or texture can be achieved. Listed below are a few ideas.

- Cast-in-place concrete can be pre-colored and then a pattern of stones, brick, tile, or cobbles can be stamped into the damp surface.

- Pre-cast concrete pavers are available in a myriad of shapes, from small rounds that look like Japanese river stones to pierced blocks designed to grow lawn in patterns. These pavers provide a durable, green surface — perfect for driveways and parking areas.
- Combining exposed aggregate of various shapes and colors with edges of brick or cobble gives a traditional look. Use granite strips for a contemporary style.

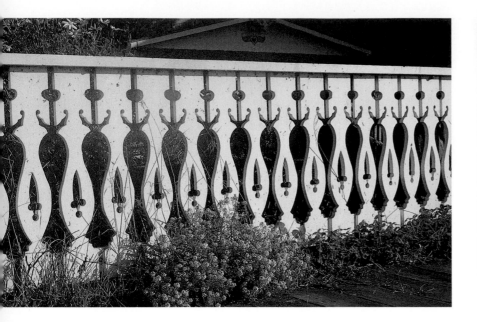

FENCES

The design of a good fence depends on the function it serves and its location. Once determined, the style of the fence can be designed according to personal aesthetics, budget, and any local building code guidelines. Most fences are constructed for security, property, and entrance definition, or for the creation of an outdoor room to provide privacy and weather protection. Fences can keep children and pets either within or outside the owner's property. Fences can also be a psychological deterrent to potential trespassers.

Common fence heights range from 3½ to 6 feet (1.1 to 1.8 meters) tall. They can be designed to be solid, semi-transparent, or transparent. Generally, if the lot size is small—as most modern residential developments are—it is desirable to keep views as open as possible. If a fence is required at the property line, keep it low and open or use hedges. City lots are an exception and often require tall, solid fences or walls for privacy and to take advantage of front yard space. Entrance fences close to the house may be solid or semi-transparent to provide privacy. Putting the fence away from the property line will not obstruct the open look of the neighborhood landscape.

The old saying, "good fences make good neighbors," is often quite true. Be certain the fence construction looks good on both sides and is an addition to and not a detraction from the neighborhood. Planting flowering evergreen shrubs, trees, or vines softens and blends the strong linear architectural lines that can be so abrupt. Raised flower beds along the fence also soften the visual impact while providing seating and more accessible gardening.

Fences can be solid or pierced, short or tall, decorative or purely functional. Facing page, clockwise: A slotted fence provides support for decorative vines ; a clump of sea lavender also helps to soften the lines; a rustic fence serves as an effective property boundary between a wooded lot and busy street, yet still allows the house to remain visible; a lattice fence establishes a private area within a large garden. Ornamental grasses and climbing roses help soften the severe architectural lines.

GATES

The entrance gateway is very symbolic, as it is the threshold from public to private space. Gates should complement the fence or wall and give the owner or designer the opportunity for an artistic garden accent. Gates can be designed to see over, to see through, or to be completely solid for privacy.

Consider the gate posts as a design element. They must be strong enough structurally to endure the added weight and stress of the gate, but the addition of well-proportioned finials—such as balls, cones, or an arch—can give the gate or fence distinction.

Gates are most commonly made from wood or wrought iron. Iron gates may be very elaborate, with detailed scrollwork on the horizontal framework and side panels. When a gate is designed to be seen through, try to place it on an axis of the garden to take full advantage of the vista.

Wooden gates can be solid, pierced with designs, or carved with garden motifs such as foliage, squirrels, rabbits, or quail. Sculptural gates are another choice and are designed in steel with cut-out shapes and patterns reminiscent of Matisse.

Structurally, gates have a square or rectangular frame. Wooden gates may require diagonal bracing from the top corner of the latch side down to the opposite corner near the hinges. Hardware such as hinges and latches should be sturdy and resistant to weather and corrosion. The width of the opening must be a minimum of 32 inches (81 centimeters), and there should be 2 feet (61 centimeters) between the opening edge of a gate and the nearest perpendicular restriction to allow for comfortable access. Gates that are both functional and aesthetic bring art and pleasure into the garden, giving subtle hints of what's to come.

A window cut into this wooden gate helps direct visitors to a side entrance (above). If the door were solid it would have a forbidding appearance. This distinctive gate (left) is a great idea when streets don't have numbers. Here visitors can be told to "look for the house with the red gate."

*T*his silver metal gate is
(right) *set into a fence of iron railings. Like the red*
gate, it has a welcoming aspect to it, yet establishes a
strong sense of privacy. A tall wooden gate set into a
high hedge (below) *establishes privacy for a shady*
sitting area. The gate allows a person to look into or out
of the sitting area.

chapter five

CLIMATE CONTROL

SIGNIFICANT changes can be made in a landscape to alter the climate in a given area. Indeed, micro-climates may already exist that can be exploited to make the garden more versatile for growing plants or for creating comfort at various times of the year. If you take a walk around your property during summer you will feel distinct temperature differences. For example, an open, sunny slope or an unshaded gravel turnaround driveway feels hot, while in the same vicinity a shady area on the north side of a stone wall or under trees, feels cool. The margin of a rocky stream or a pond surrounded by grass is a good deal cooler than an open meadow or a parking lot.

Scoop up a handful of soil in full sun after a week without rainfall, and most likely it feels dust-dry; in the same area soil under a shaded layer of leaves feels moist and cool. For plants, the temperature of the *soil* may be much more important than the temperature of the *atmosphere*.

A good time of year to detect microclimates around the home is in winter, especially after heavy frost or snowfall. Notice where the ice and snow melt first, indicating sun traps, and where the ice and snow last a long time, indicating cold spots.

Some micro-climates are all too easily altered. Cut down a grove of trees or replace a green lawn with concrete paving, and a cool, refreshing environment is transformed into one that is uncomfortably hot and dry. Replace a living hedge with a stucco wall, and the reflected light and heat may be unbearable for most plants.

Conditions inside a house are also affected by landscape features. A windbreak of evergreen pines can cushion the force of cold winds and reduce heating bills. An overhanging tree may be so overgrown it can make rooms dark and gloomy. Following are some desirable forms of climate control.

SUN TRAPS

Given the choice, most people would rather have lots of sun than lots of shade. Sunshine is vital, not only for the health of people, but also for the growth of most plants. Experiments in light laboratories have shown that even one percent more light can make one hundred percent difference in plant growth. A tree that shades a vegetable garden at mid-day can prevent the proper ripening of warm-weather crops

such as tomatoes, eggplants, and melons. Yet the removal of a single branch may allow enough sunlight to penetrate for successful harvests.

Perhaps the most popular forms of sun traps are lean-to greenhouses and sunrooms attached to the house, with a southern or easterly exposure. Rooms with lots of glass (for example, with French windows) can heat up with amazing speed, just like a parked car with all its windows closed. In winter, this solar heat can be directed into the house by means of a fan. At night, when outside temperatures plummet, heat can be retained in waterstorage containers painted black or commercially available solar tubes filled with heat-retaining compounds.

In summer, when the heat in a glassroom can be oppressive, various devices can be used to produce cool conditions, including shades, vents that open automatically, recirculating fans, water fountains, and air conditioning. Where the room needs shading, it's best to break the sun's rays *before* they reach the glass by placing the shades on the outside. Bamboo roller blinds, cloth shades, and aluminum blinds are excellent and inexpensive ways to block the sun. Silverbacked custom blinds made for solariums both reflect excess light when closed on a hot day and retain the captured radiant heat for cool evenings. These blinds provide privacy from the outside but are semi-transparent from indoors looking out.

A *lean-to greenhouse attached to the south side of a house* (facing page) *becomes a sun trap, allowing the owner to grow exotic plants. Magnolia and dogwood trees provide shade during the spring and summer so the greenhouse does not overheat.* Right: *Bright sunlight is also important for these sun-loving annuals. Concrete paths and brick terraces lead up to this patio area* (far right) *fully exposed to the sun. If shade is required, a large portable umbrella can be erected.* Below: *In this design by the Brickman Group, a sunny deck projects over a pair of ponds, joined by a waterfall. A low, wide rail prevents people from accidentally stepping over the side.*

Another popular type of sun trap is a sunbathing area—with or without a swimming pool. For maximum tanning effect, an area for sunbathing should have a bright, reflective surface, such as smooth white beach pebbles that are comfortable for bare feet. White walls will reflect more light and provide privacy.

Afternoon sun is a good deal more intense than morning sun; therefore a sun trap facing slightly southwest will be warmer than one facing southeast. This is good to remember when making a bed for plants that like the heat, including waterlilies, cacti and succulents, tender fruit trees such as figs and citrus, and many flowering vines such as trumpetcreeper, honeysuckle, and bougainvillea.

A climbing hydrangea vine (below) establishes a rich decorative canopy above this colonnade, while a creeping vine (right) creates a shaded area along this garden path.

CREATING SHADE

In summer, temperatures throughout most of the United States and Canada rise into the nineties. With little wind and high humidity, this heat can be intensely uncomfortable. The first steps towards creating comfort are shade and adequate air movement. Shade can be provided by natural elements like trees and vines, or by manmade structures like awnings, umbrellas, arbors, summerhouses, gazebos, pavilions, and grottos.

Trees and vines have green leaves which reduce glare on hazy and cloudless days. Leaves are also nature's own air conditioners, composed mostly of moisture drawn from the soil. Thus, the air temperature in the shade of a tree can be 10 to 15 degrees lower than in an unshaded area. A tree's leaf canopy is composed of layers of branches with spaces between the leaves, providing good air circulation. Before deciding what kind of tree to plant for shade, consider its profile. Trees with spreading branches, like silk trees and scarlet maples, provide better shade than more upright trees, like poplars and arborvitae. Also, trees with fine leaves, like honey locusts and silk trees, allow grass to grow under them better than trees with dense tree canopies, like oaks and sycamores.

When trees or canopies are to be placed close to the house to shade a room in summer, it's important to realize that in winter the sun travels low on the horizon. Therefore, a short overhang may be more desirable than one that extends far out into the garden. It will shade a room in summer and allow sunlight to flood the room in winter, when radiant heat is welcome.

When choosing a shade tree for the

garden or patio, consider several points: *the tree's mature shape* (Does it form a canopy?); *growth habits* (Is it fast or slow? What's the size at maturity?); *root system* (Is it agressive, like a willow, which will seek water in your plumbing, or does it have high surface roots that can heave up patios, make mowing difficult or become an obstacle to trip over?); *the mess from the tree* (dropping fruits or shedding large amounts of leaves will litter the patio and lawn); and *water requirements* (If planted in a lawn or flowerbed, can the tree take frequent surface water?)

Another consideration when choosing trees for shade is the possibilty of pollarding and pleaching for extra decorative appeal. Pollarding is a pruning technique whereby side braches are pruned away to make a straight trunk, and upper branches are cut back to the top of the trunk. In many trees this stimulates a flush of dense, bushy foliage growth, like a "top-knot," which is easily shaped into a square or mound—helping to decorate monotonous expanses of wood or masonry. Popular trees for this treatment are catalpa, linden, beech, hornbeam, maple, and sycamore.

A "lath house" can be strictly functional—a shaded area of wooden slats to keep house plants healthy during summer—or purely decorative, garlanded with vines and used to display exotic hanging baskets, as it is here (top). A metal arbor (above) guides visitors from one garden space to another. Vines produce a tunnel effect and a shady retreat. A thatched summerhouse (left) provides a pleasant place to pause and rest during a stroll in this richly planted perennial garden.

PROVIDING COOL SPACES

Though shade helps to create a cool environment, it is not the only factor. "Green gardens" are popular throughout the Southern states, utilizing boxwood to create enclosures, hosta and lily turf to make ground covers, turf grass to cover open spaces, a fountain or pool to add a cooling accent, and flagstone to make overlooking paths or terraces. Besides the cooling effect green plants have in the landscape, green also provides a psychological coolness; green is on the cool side of the color wheel (red is opposite on the hot side). If the green garden space is bounded by a brick or stone wall, English ivy may be used to reduce the reflected glare.

In addition to flagstone, large boulders can lower temperatures, as can any kind of flowing water—particularly water running along a stream, flume, or rill.

Boulders and rock steps
(above, far left) *can help establish a cooling influence.*
A multitude of cooling features establish a highly
decorative shade garden. Here (below, far left), *the*
shade-loving ferns, hosta, and ivy establish a rich
tapestry of soothing colors; the brick path and stone
pedestal complete the cooling effect. Left: *The gradual*
transition from woodland to lawn is made by means of a
grassy path bordered by shade-loving pachysandra, and
a small orchard of dwarf fruit trees. Besides using trees
to provide a cool place within a garden, water too, is an
important element. (Above right) *A small, simple pool*
has a shaded deck around it. This circular garden bench
(below right) *surrounding a tulip tree makes a pleasant*
place to sit and enjoy the dappled shade.

Sunken spaces can be used to help channel air movement and cool an area. For example, over most of the United States prevailing winds blow from the west. Therefore, creating a gap in a hedge or a line of trees can help channel breezes to a particular place in the garden. Slopes are especially good devices to direct air, since cool air naturally flows downhill. An idyllic place to establish a sitting area is a low spot where cool air is trapped by enclosures such as hedges or walls in the shape of a semicircle or open-ended square.

Wooded decks or stone terraces which project over water create cool sitting areas. The flow of water creates breezes and lowers the temperature. Even more effective is a stone shelter—such as a springhouse or grotto—with a channel of water inside. Though these are not comfortable places to spend extended periods of time, stone shelters make wonderful landscape accents and serve as storage places for perishable commodities, such as wine.

SHELTERING

The most common elements from which shelters provide protection are heavy rains, wind, and salt spray. For good protection from rain consider canopies, such as umbrellas and arbors formed by trees or man-made structures. Hedges, windbreak trees, fences, and walls help ensure protection from wind and salt spray. By far the most effective windbreaks are evergreen trees and hedges, since they cushion the force of winds far more effectively than a solid barrier. If you need protection from salt spray be sure to choose plants that can resist both the force of high winds and heavy salt spray. On exposed sites, the biggest problem is how to establish a shelter belt that isn't likely to blow away itself. Frequently, a temporary, man-made structure may be needed until the shelter plants are well-established. A wall of hay bales, rolls of burlap stapled to strong posts, bamboo screens, and rough fences made from bundles of reeds or branches are the most effective means to protect a line of shrubs or young trees.

In extreme situations, establish a double line of protective trees and shrubs. For example, a line of pines might form a tall barrier as the first line of defense, while as a second line, a billowing hedge of Russian olive or *pittosporum* forms a wide, low screen.

*E*nglish boxwood (left) *is a popular evergreen windbreak that has a billowy, informal appearance when left unpruned. Russian olive* (above) *is a popular windbreak in seaside gardens because it is tolerant of high winds and salt spray. This evergreen hemlock hedge* (above right) *has an archway cut into it to provide access to a sheltered perennial garden.*

EVERGREEN WINDBREAK TREES

Asterisked varieties are salt tolerant:
Abies species (Fir trees)
*Casuarina cunninghamiana (Australian pine)
Chamaecyparis lawsoniana (Lawson False cypress)
Cupressocyparis leylandii (Leyland cypress)
*Cupressus macrocarpa (Monterey cypress)
Oleo europa (Olive)
Picea abies (Norway spruce)
Pinus radiata (Monterey pine)
Pinus strobus (White pine)
*Pinus sylvestris (Scotch pine)
*Pinus thunbergiana (Japanese black pine)
Podocarpus macrophyllus (Japanese yew)
*Quercus robur (English oak)
Taxus species (yews)
Thuja occidentalis (American white cedar)
Tsuga canadensis (Hemlock)
Eucalyptus species
*Ilex species (Holly)
Juniperus virginiana (Red cedar)

EVERGREEN HEDGES

Asterisked varieties are salt tolerant:
Buxus sempervirens (English boxwood)
*Carissa grandiflora (Natal plum)
*Choisya species
*Crataegus species (Hawthorn)
*Hibiscus rosa-sinensis (Chinese hibiscus)
*Hippophae rhamnoides (Sea Buckthorn)
*Hydrangea species (Hydrangeas)
*Myrtus species (Myrtles)
Nerium oleander (oleander)
Osmanthus species (False hollies)
Pinus mugo mugo (Mugo pine)
*Pittosporum tobiria (Mock orange)
Prunus laurocerasus (English laurel)
Raphiolepis indica (Indian Hawthorn)
Rhododendron species (*Rhododendrons & Azaleas*)
*Rosa rugosa (Rugosa rose)
Viburnum species (Viburnum)
Weigela florida (Weigela)

chapter six

CREATING PRIVACY

A SPECIAL, secluded place is a welcome retreat for even the most outgoing people. Privacy in the landscape can be created unobtrusively by using carefully placed trees, hedges, and vines and by taking advantage of natural topographical features, such as a turn in the path, a depression in a meadow, or a slight hill or berm. In addition, fences, walls, or treillage, provide structural privacy.

SCREENS AND DIVIDERS

Screens and dividers of various designs and materials may be employed to separate garden areas without obstructing views. Redwood louvered dividers or accent screens of wrought iron grillwork or pierced tilework make handsome dividers that still allow the passage of light and air. If more flexibility is desired, a view divider can be adapted from the Japanese soji screen. Durable screens (made from opaque white fiberglass panels framed with bamboo or redwood), canvas awnings, and ripstop nylon curtains of any color imaginable work well for seasonal use.

A screen or divider may be high or low, airy or solid. It may be used to hide storage spaces, separate play yards, conceal vegetable or compost areas, or to create privacy for sunbathers, spa-soakers, or outdoor entertaining. A divider makes for visual interest; it provides a background for special plantings and enhances a deep garden by dividing the space so it can't all be seen at once. A screen can be a beautiful garden feature itself—a Japanese folk art screen woven from bamboo or a stained glass window set into a wooden frame—or purely functional, providing protection from wind and curious onlookers.

Facing page, above:
Bougainvillea vines help to camouflage this utility area adjoining a California residence. Facing page, below: This Japanese-style fence of woven bamboo stands on a low stone wall, effectively screening a busy highway and providing a pleasant place for the eye to rest. Above left, above right, and left: Light wood screens, treillage, and grape stake fences provide privacy while allowing breezes and dappled sunlight to pass through. Sometimes, privacy is only an illusion that creates a cozier, more intimate enclosure that discourages neighbors and passersby from peering in.

WALLS AND FENCES

Walls and fences can be used to ensure privacy and to permanently enclose outdoor spaces that feel too vast and open to be comfortable. In small gardens where space is at a premium, fences take up far less room than hedges or walls.

In a city garden, security, privacy, and protection from the street can be accomplished by a solid wall or fence at the property line. The wall or fence should blend with the house's architecture, using similar materials of wood, brick, stone, or stucco. An iron gate would allow a glimpse into a formalized entry court, while a solid wooden gate provides even more privacy. Vines of roses, clematis, bougainvillea, or

Virginia creeper help soften the hard lines of a wall. The effect can be formalized by training ivy to grow in a diamond pattern or by placing matching sentinels of specimen plants, statues, or other ornamentation on either side of the gateway.

For added height, plant trees along the fence or wall so that the tree trunks form a column—the heads can be trimmed to form a neat screen above the wall. Another way to increase height is to add lattice and grow vines above the fence. This gives an airy, softer look, and the enclosed area forms an entrance court, utilizing front yard space and providing shelter and privacy. Espaliered sasanqua camellias, ferns, and azaleas work well in a shady courtyard, while where there is plenty of sun, espaliered fruit trees and herbs can create a formal European kitchen garden.

An imaginative fence design is further embellished by espaliered fruit trees and a low flower border. This modern wooden fence (facing page, below) by California landscape architect Garrett Eckbo, screens his property from his neighbors. This brick wall (above) is adorned by a free-flowering variety of trumpet creeper, turning an austere barrier into a beautiful landscape feature. Top right: A city garden in the historic section of Charleston, South Carolina, has a fortress-like brick wall and strong iron gate, ensuring excellent security; yet, the property has a friendly quality, partly because the open grillwork permits a good view of the garden beyond the wall, and because of the Lady Banks rose spilling over the top. Brick walls (right) are made less austere by capping the top with curved bricks or by changing the height, especially on a slope.

HEDGES, TREES, AND VINES

Hedges, trees, and vines can be planted, trimmed, and trained into "green architecture" that dominates a landscape or in softer, more natural ways that blend. Either way, they create privacy around or within a landscape, while adding greatly to the garden's beauty.

A variety of shrubs, deciduous trees, and evergreens planted in a seemingly random pattern (with thought given to foliage, flower, bark and berry color, and texture) creates a natural screen, which looks like woodland. This kind of planting occupies more of the garden's square footage, but since it blends into the landscape and doesn't form a visual boundary it creates a feeling of space.

Double or triple rows of clipped hedges of different heights, color tones, and textures form an interesting border screen or frame for the front of the house. If the short hedge borders the sidewalk and the taller one is closer to the house, they'll provide the desired effect of enclosure and still allow sidewalk pedestrians some elbow room. Plan for an access path of at least 18 to 24 inches (30 to 61 centimeters) between the hedges for maintenance, feeding, and pruning.

Trees and vines trained on arbors, pergolas, or wire provide privacy from neighbors who might otherwise be able to look down into the garden. They also provide the secure feeling of a "roof" overhead. Vines grown on treillage offer an airy screen. Trees can be planted in *allées* and pleached to direct views or strategically placed to create privacy in designated parts of the landscape. Yew and cypress trees are most responsive to heavy pruning, creating solid walls that can include windows, niches, arches, columns, or animal shapes. Holly, privet, choisya, Eugenia, and pittosporums make excellent hedges and screens and are relatively fast-growing.

*T*his red and white azalea hedge (facing page, above) *creates a spectacular effect. The same pattern can be achieved using shrubs with green and bronze foliage. This hedge of American beech* (facing page, below) *has been trained over a wire form to create a beautiful natural archway. Vines covering a wide expanse of wall* (above left) *make a sheltered place to sit outdoors and rest or entertain. A flowering wisteria vine* (above right) *decorates the entrance to a house on this busy San Francisco street. A billowing hedge of Robin Hood roses* (right) *makes a good, informal, property divider.*

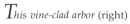This vine-clad arbor (right) creates a private, shaded space beside a swimming pool. Below left: Here, fancy ironwork is used to divide this back terrace into individual private spaces, while an island bed planted with azaleas, flowering dogwood, and pansies (below right) helps to give the space more privacy.

PRIVACY WITHIN THE SPACE

Privacy within a garden space is created with plantings, structures, and the "lay of the land." If your site is flat, consider having some grading done to create a more interesting rolling landscape. Soil can be brought in, or if you are digging a pool or pond use the excess dirt to form a berm, raised beds, slopes, or a sunken garden. With a varied topography not all of the landscape will be visible at once, giving the designer many opportunities for secret gardens, secluded niches, and surprise elements. A ribbon-like garden path can lead to or away from a special place. A labyrinth of hedges, screens, or masonry walls may create winding passages to a hidden place within the garden—a quiet, private place of solitude.

Above: A wooden arbor with facing seats provides extra privacy in an enclosed garden space. A cozy nook tucked into the corner of a wall (below), and a hedge, establish an inviting place to find privacy for reading or meditation.

Chapter seven

OPTICAL ILLUSIONS

ILLUSIONS

are used in gardens to create a focus, expand the feeling of size, create depth, provide intimacy, and divert attention from or camouflage negative aspects. A bit of theatrical, carefully staged "make believe" can supply a welcome solution to a problem of space. The French are masters of *trompe l'oeil* (trick of the eye). In the seventeenth and eighteenth centuries they skillfully developed this technique in garden design by using forced perspectives in trellis work, painted murals, and mirrors, and by fore-shortened flower beds, lawns, walks, and vistas. These same techniques can be applied to landscape designs today. For example, Thomas Church adapts many *trompe l'oeil* techniques successfully to give the illusion of distance to the small city gardens he designs.

ADDING DEPTH

Most inner-city or suburban gardens suffer from lack of depth. The lot size is usually small and so clearly defined by fences, neighboring houses, apartments, or roads that the viewer is constantly aware of the limited space of the garden and has little desire to explore further. There are many *trompe l'oeil* techniques that can be used to solve these limitations.

Just as a mirrored wall in a living room or department store gives the illusion of a great deal more space and light, so can carefully placed mirrors be used in the landscape—set in a brick or wooden wall as a series of mirrored arches.

The mirrors can be positioned to repeat pleasing views and vistas, to multiply a perennial flower bed, to endlessly continue a line of trees, or reflect back a city skyline. Mirrors can also be placed at either end of a long, straight reflecting pool to give it an infinite quality or used as a background for statuary at the end of a focal point. When mirrors are used outside, it is important to set them above ground level to avoid moisture. A special mirror sealer by *Layal* is available from glass and mirror specialists, which—when applied on the edges and surface—will help prevent moisture from getting inside and blackening the silver backing. Mirrors add much reflected light to the garden, so plant with this in mind.

Trompe l'oeil treillage uses exaggerated, forced perspective lines to focus on a statue or painted scenery. This creates

Depth can be added to a vista in many different ways. A narrow walkway (facing page, above) and vertical accents created by columnar evergreens and topiary cones, or (facing page, below) a well-defined, narrow brick path accentuated with dwarf chipped boxwood and an archway are only a few of the ways to create depth. A confined narrow space (right) behind a townhouse looks larger than it actually is by a division of spaces; the central rectangular lawn area is sandwiched between two, shady garden spaces.

great depth in a tiny 10-foot-square (3-meter-square) courtyard or a long, narrow space. Accurate craftsmanship, careful planning, and a good sense of scale are essential to produce a successful illusion.

There is much to learn from landscape painters about creating an illusion. These artists rely heavily on the use of light, shade, tone, color, and shape placement to give a two-dimensional canvas perspective and depth. Landscape designers employ the painter's techniques with the additional advantage of three-dimensional space. When laying out a canvas or garden using forced perspective, decide on the vantage point. From what location will the garden be viewed the most? Will it be the terrace or the living room window? Le Norte had the major vistas in Versailles radiate from the upstairs bed chamber of Louis the XIV.

Monet's greatest view is from his front door, straight down the Grande Allée, through a tunnel of rose-covered arches to a blue-green gate at the focal point.

Warm and hot colors such as reds, oranges, gold, hot pink, and bright yellow come forward. A painter applies these colors to the foreground; and the landscaper plants the same colors close to the vantage point. Blue tends to appear more distant (many landscape artists paint distant mountains pale blue or lavender), so blue flowers and blue-green foliage blended with lavender, mauve, and soft pink are often best planted towards the back of the garden. Another painterly technique is to use large shapes in the foreground with smaller or more finely textured objects receding. Landscape designers add to the sense of perspective by putting large, deeply-colored foliaged plants (like canthus or hostas) closer to the view with the texture of the plants gradually getting finer and perhaps paler in color farther from the view. Small plants, such as dianthus and bluish grasses, and trees such as blue cedars and birches give the impression of greater distance.

Another way to add depth to a landscape is to use flower borders, grass panels, and walkways that are wider in the foreground and gradually become narrower as they get farther from the house. How much narrower depends on the total length and width of the garden. Lay out a design with stakes and string to get an idea of how it will look. It may look better to have the bed only two feet narrower, or you may prefer to really exaggerate the layout like a *trompe l'oeil* trellis.

Far left: *Containers of exotic plants clustered around the edges of an enclosed brick patio create this cozy outdoor dining area. A large rock draped with plants and an informal stone seat (left) blend perfectly into their surroundings. Dense planting over a large area (below) creates a rich tapestry of soft colors and textures. A bench nestled in an intimate corner invites visitors to sit and enjoy the waterlily pool.*

CREATING COZINESS

A feeling of coziness can be achieved by providing a more human scale to wide-open spaces. Dividing up one large space into intimate and private garden rooms—about the same size as corresponding rooms in the house—will make the garden more useable for dining, entertaining, relaxing, and other activities. Vignettes of different colors or moods can be designed to be seen from indoors. The variety will create coziness and simultaneously give an impression of more space. Framing landscape views and vistas with architectural or horticultural arches, doorways, or windows creates coziness without causing a cramped feeling. Providing a "ceiling" effect 8 to 12 feet (2.5 to 3.7 meters) high over part of the garden with a canopy of tree boughs, latticework, canvas awnings, arbors, bamboo screens, vines, or wire also contributes to a cozy, nest-like feeling.

Drama can be created in many different ways: In this bas-relief (right), Medusa's head provides a dramatic focus to this walled-in garden and (below left) an enlarged statue of David holding the head of Goliath are both unexpected features in a woodland garden. Below right: Plants, too, can be very dramatic; this Agave (A.americana variegata), is a dramatic accent in Luther Burbank's California home. The addition of nightlighting would greatly increase this effort.

DRAMA

Dramatic illusion can be accomplished in the landscape much the way it is done on a theatrical stage—with lighting, forced perspective, color choice, and painted murals used to give a *faux* (false, fake) finish to something uninteresting, and with the unexpected surprise accent.

At night, lighting can be used to produce shadow gardens with exquisite, silhouetted traceries on walls and walkways. Reflections on water sparkle and bounce and are exaggerated with dramatic lighting. A sculpture of neon lights comes alive after dark, awakening a quiet corner of the garden.

For the visitor who walks into the garden towards the focal point, create a surprise element off to the side—some small detail that can not be seen until come upon. Perhaps the unexpected will be a small pool with aquatic plants or a change in the color scheme or plant type.

ACCENTS

Carefully placed garden accents can help create the illusion of more space in a narrow backyard lot. Consider the classical use of a terminal point of architectural interest at the end of the garden axis. This draws the eye down the length of the garden to the fountain, gazebo, bench, birdbath, gate, or *trompe l'oeil* treillage.

When smaller accents are placed on either side of the focal point so that they interrupt the distance but do not obscure the view, it takes longer for the viewer's eye to move down the garden, making it appear larger. Urns, statues, large pots of specimen plants, or a series of arches placed at the edges of the axis work well. In French gardens, cone-shaped shrubs are used liberally to punctuate the vistas. If a solid line is drawn next to a broken line of the same length, it takes the eye longer to follow the broken line. Placing accents along a walk creates the same illusion. To increase this illusion, place the accent plants closer together as they go further back, and design the walk to narrow as it recedes.

Carefully placed, garden accents can be used to create an illusion of depth or simply to add an interesting focus. Above: This bronze sculpture of a woman with a water jug is appropriate beside a swimming pool. Above right: This Bavarian-style birdhouse adds a fanciful accent to this wildflower garden. Right: This terra-cotta rooster with succulents cascading down its back adds a bit of whimsy to this sunny wall.

*G*arden accents can utilize

things found in the garden itself. Above left: *Here's a*

great idea for enhancing a fence post—attach a birdhouse

to the top of the post and plant the base with morning

glories and sunflowers.

107

A cast iron "tree" (left) holds pots of variegated ivy camouflaging a stucco wall. Below left: A privet surrounds an unsightly fire hydrant, hiding it completely from a nearby sitting area. Below right: An arch made of latticework helps to enhance an otherwise monotonous expanse of brick. Facing page, above left: A wooden enclosure helps to hide trash containers in a small townhouse garden. Facing page, above right: An elaborate tromp l'oeil trellis on the stucco wall adds depth, focus, and a lovely accent to this French-style garden. Facing page, below: The glare of a stucco wall is softened by English ivy trained as espaliers.

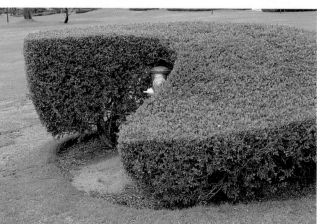

CAMOUFLAGE

There are often many negative aspects of a garden that cannot be changed but that benefit from a little camouflage. If the back of your garden ends with a dominating wall, consider the following ideas:

- Paint the wall a color that will tend to recede or a color that will complement your garden.
- Paint a *trompe l'oeil* mural that continues the landscape.
- Paint a *faux* finish to complement the garden—perhaps a stone, marble, or stucco wall.
- Nail an attractive door on the wall, and create an entryway illusion.
- Plant vines like Virginia creeper to cover the wall.
- Plant a thick, mixed hedge, and place an attractive garden gate in it.
- Place a *trompe l'oeil* treillage on the wall as a focal point.

chapter eight

CONDUCTING MOVEMENT

MOVEMENT

is an essential part of a successful landscape design. It can be achieved by the
actual walkways in the garden or by transitions between various spaces. Also, paths,
steps, stairs, ramps, stepping stones,
bridges, tunnels, *allées*, corridors, and pergolas can be used to conduct and facilitate
movement. Another way to introduce movement in the landscape is to employ various

visual effects. Curves used in paths, patios, walks, borders, and beds create leisurely movement and rhythm. Fountains, streams, waterfalls, cascades, and rills supply enduring visual and auditory stimuli, while masses of tall decorative grasses, drifts of bulbs, weeping willows, and birches, or other plants that look graceful in a breeze, help accentuate movement.

PATHS

Paths are narrow, informal trails that tend to make less of a visual impact in the landscape than "walks," which are more dominant and structured. Often paths are made

by constant foot traffic wearing a shortcut across a lawn or through ground covers and hedges. Paths can be established after they have been informally created by use, or they can be planned to connect different areas of the garden—the greenhouse to the potting bench, the back kitchen door to the compost pile and trash cans, or the children's playhouse to the swing-set. Paths also allow access to spots between flowers in the cutting garden or between hedges for pruning, and they can create a connecting ribbon around specimen plants, garden features, or to a special view.

Paths encourage people to wander and explore. They can be laid out to create a

sequence of events—to glimpse a statue or terminal point and then double back or turn—coaxing the visitor into a game of hide-and-seek with the landscape.

The texture of the path's surface dictates the way it is used. A smooth surface quickens the pace and is easy to traverse. Coarser, smaller, uneven surfaces (like cobblestone and rough tile) slow the pace and can be used to indicate areas intended for special purposes, such as an entrance or place to relax. Coarse, loose material (such as gravel, wood chips, and oyster shells) makes the slowest surface to walk on and is noisy when you do. Some homeowners feel the sound is a deterrant to trespassers.

*P*aths can be created from many different materials and serve a multitude of purposes. A path of used brick (facing page, left) *laid with annuals and perennials, creates this informal design. In a formal garden (facing page, right),* a *gravel path is made less austere by an arbor festooned with Lady Banks roses.* Above: *Swirls of rough stone blocks create an appealing informal design. In this path* (right), *the pattern draws the visitor into the garden.*

F̲ar left: *Shrubs pruned in this manner have a soothing influence, like cushions of moss, making a suitable contrast to the rough stone steps.* Left: *Rough stone risers and gravel treads ascend a hillside rock garden; flowering plants spill over the edges to soften the look of the stone.* Below left: *Flat stone slabs make effective steps in a woodland garden.* Facing page, right: *This raised deck with wooden steps, by the Brickman Group, has been placed at the bottom of a suburban garden as a quiet place to sit and entertain guests.* Facing page, far right: *This brick path negotiates a gentle slope by means of narrow risers and long treads.* Facing page, below right: *With landscape ties for risers and gravel for treads, this design by the Brickman Group is made even more attractive by the introduction of boulders along the sides and clumps of hosta and ferns in the crevices.*

STEPS

Broad, graceful steps are a strong design element, providing an excellent, smooth transition from patio to lawn or between other elevations of garden rooms. Broad steps can make comfortable extra seating when you entertain, and they offer a perfect display place for potted plants. The first step can be designed to blend into the patio, changing surface material, for example, from an aggregate patio to brick steps. The last step can be set into the ground level and broadened to form an edge or landing. Most home landscapes only ac-

cept six broad steps as a design feature before they become too dominant.

STAIRS

Stairs work well in the home landscape to provide access to an upper deck, terrace, or the house. A garden stairway can have wider tread and shorter risers than a stairway indoors, where space is at more of a premium (refer to chart). Materials include stone, brick, wood, or cement. For steps that will be used often, safety is as important a design consideration as aesthetics. Non-slip surfaces, a handrail, and good lighting for night use are essential safety features. It is good to provide a landing every 10 to 12 steps to be used as a place to catch your breath, as a deck for sunning, or as a spot to stop and admire a view. Railings are unnecessary where the grade change is less than 4½ feet (1.4 meters) and access for elderly or disabled people is not required.

Earth steps carved into the hillside do not last long and are impassable in heavy rains and snow, but they can create a romantic path to a beach or woodland. If the garden terrain is very rocky, steps can be cut into the natural stone.

RAMPS

Ramps provide a design alternative to stairways and steps and can be incorporated alongside steps to accommodate a variety of needs. Any surface pitched more than 5 degrees is considered a ramp. The gradient should be no more than 1:12 and the surface smooth enough to allow for easy ascent. People who find steps difficult, such as the elderly, disabled, or wheelchair users, need ramps to reach places that are otherwise inaccessible. Ramps are also useful for wheeled vehicles such as bicycles, wheelbarrows, lawnmowers, and baby strollers. The main disadvantage of a ramp, however, is that it usually takes up more space than steps do. If an elevation is steep, use a right-angled ramp or switchback ramp with a 5-foot-square (1.5-meter-square) landing at the turn.

RAMPS FOR OUTDOOR USE

1. Straight-Run

2. Angled Landing

3. Intermediate/Switch-Back Landing

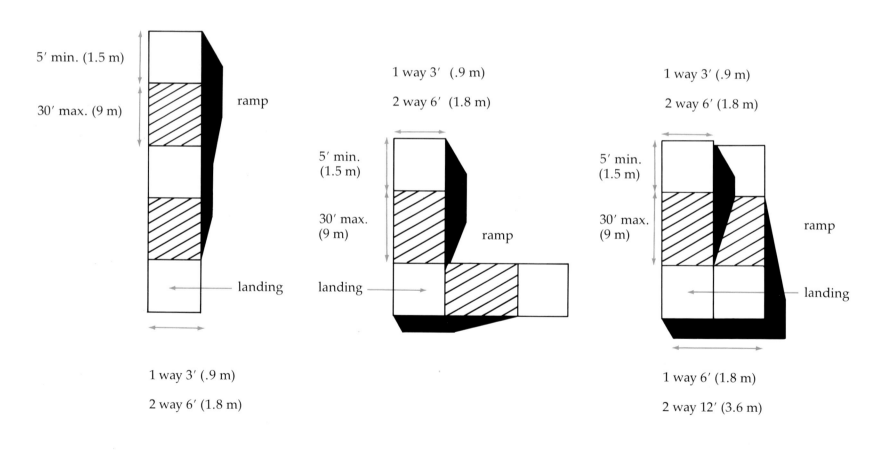

1. Straight-Run

5′ min. (1.5 m)

30′ max. (9 m)

ramp

landing

1 way 3′ (.9 m)

2 way 6′ (1.8 m)

2. Angled Landing

1 way 3′ (.9 m)

2 way 6′ (1.8 m)

5′ min. (1.5 m)

30′ max. (9 m)

ramp

landing

3. Intermediate/Switch-Back Landing

1 way 3′ (.9 m)

2 way 6′ (1.8 m)

5′ min. (1.5 m)

30′ max. (9 m)

ramp

landing

1 way 6′ (1.8 m)

2 way 12′ (3.6 m)

■ Ramps should be designed to carry a minimum live load of 100 lbs (45.5 kg) per square foot.

Handrails for Ramps

Handrails for Stairways

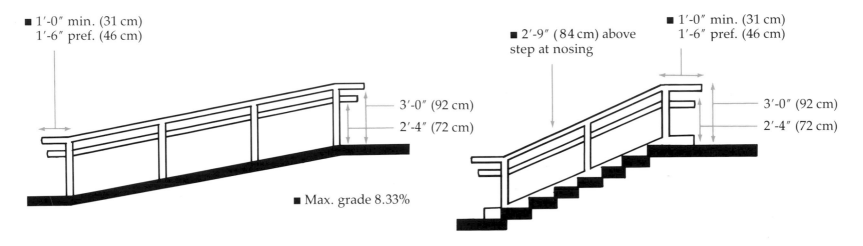

- 1'-0" min. (31 cm)
  1'-6" pref. (46 cm)

- 2'-9" (84 cm) above
  step at nosing

- 1'-0" min. (31 cm)
  1'-6" pref. (46 cm)

3'-0" (92 cm)
2'-4" (72 cm)

3'-0" (92 cm)
2'-4" (72 cm)

- Max. grade 8.33%

HANDRAILS FOR RAMPS AND STAIRS

Handrails are primarily used to provide assistance to people climbing or descending stairs or ramps, while railings are designed to prevent people from falling off dangerous areas (such as decks and balconies) and to prevent entrance to areas that are off limits.

Things to Consider When Building a Handrail:

1) For maximum safety, handrails should be provided on both sides of the stairway or ramp, especially when it is used frequently in both directions. This also gives symmetry to the design.

2) Handrails for stairs should be 2 feet 9 inches high (84 centimeters) (from the nose of the treads to the top of the handrail).

3) Handrails for ramps should be 3 feet to 3 feet 3 inches (91 centimeters to 1 meter) from the ramp surface to the top of the rail.

4) A second lower rail is helpful to children and wheelchair users. Where there are two rails on stairs or ramps, the top one should be placed at 3 feet to 3 feet 3 inches (91 centimeters to 1 meter) and the lower rail placed at 2 feet 4 inches (71 centimeters).

5) Handrails must be constructed from a smooth material that will not splinter. Wood is fine if sanded and maintained.

6) Handrails for stairs should extend 2 to 3½ feet (61 centimeters to 1 meter) past the step tread at the top and bottom, unless the extension creates a hazard.

7) Handrails on ramps should extend 1 to 1½ feet (30 to 46 centimeters) past the "heel and toe" of the ramp.

8) The extension of the railing can be curled, notched, or rounded into a ball to add design interest and offer a tactile clue to a person about to make the last step.

9) Handrails should be continuous across landings.

10) Handrails should be designed to support 250 pounds (114 kilograms) and must be kept securely fastened at all times.

*F*eatured on these pages are examples of ramps and steps with hand rails made of wood or metal. Sometimes the plantings around these structures are busy with collections of different plants, creating a leafy, intimate passageway or a spacious flower garden; in other cases, the embellishment is much simpler.

OUTDOOR STEP TYPES

Shadowline ¾″ (2 cm) max.

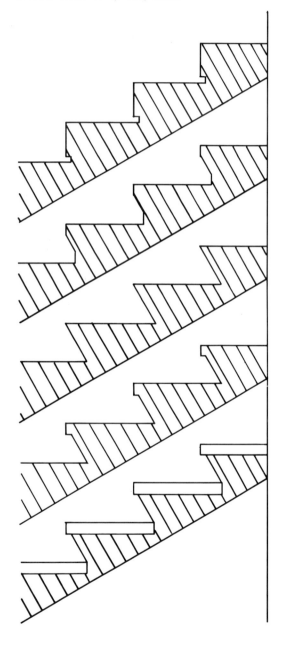

1. Acceptable if shadowline is kept to minimum.

2. Acceptable if nosing is provided with 45° bevel below.

3. Acceptable.

4. Not acceptable; recesses can catch toe of shoes, etc.

5. Open treads not acceptable for same reasons as above.

Drawings and list provided from: "Barrier Free Site Design" U.S. Dept. of Housing and Urban Development, Office of Policy Development and Research and A.S.L.A. Foundation.

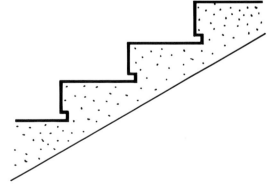

Outdoor Steps Rules of Thumb

a) 2 risers + 1 tread = 26″–27″ (66–69 cm)

b) max. riser height = 6½″ (16.6 cm)

c) min. tread depth = 11″ (28 cm)

OUTDOOR LANDINGS FOR STAIRS

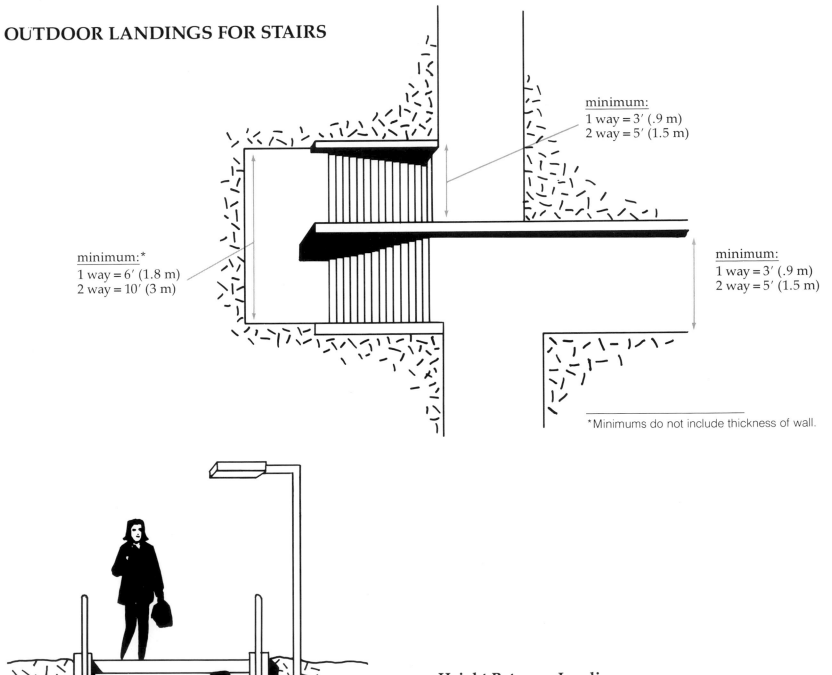

minimum:
1 way = 3′ (.9 m)
2 way = 5′ (1.5 m)

minimum:*
1 way = 6′ (1.8 m)
2 way = 10′ (3 m)

minimum:
1 way = 3′ (.9 m)
2 way = 5′ (1.5 m)

*Minimums do not include thickness of wall.

6′-0″
(1.8 m)
max.

Height Between Landings

■ Provide 5′ (1.5 m) foot-candles lighting on stair and landing areas.

■ Where total grade change exceeds 6′-0″ (1.8 m), intermediate landings are necessary.

■ Provide landings at 4′-0″ (1.2 m) intervals.

■ Landings may provide space for informal seating, or container plant display.

STEPPING-STONES

Stepping-stones can be laid out in various patterns to conduct both eye and foot movement through a tranquil garden. The Japanese are masters of carefully chosen and placed stepping-stones—in streams, across raked gravel, as islands in mossy ground covers, or set across a lawn.

Stepping-stones can be formed from many materials with various colors, textures, shapes, and styles. The flatter the surface, the easier it is to walk on. Make sure each stone is solidly set, so it won't tip or rock when stepped on. If the stones are not large enough for both feet place them in pairs, and be sure they are comfortably spaced.

For best effect, the stepping-stones should blend into the landscape, complementing its style and mood. Choose carefully the material you will use—granite slabs, flagstone, cement rounds, square blocks, redwood rounds or tiles—as well as their color, texture, shape, and placement. When possible, use materials that are indigenous to the area. Locally quarried stone will be ''at home'' in the landscape, blending easily with soil color and native plants. It may also be less expensive than imported rock, because of shipping costs. Lava rock looks natural and beautiful in tropical Hawaiian landscapes but hopelessly out of place and absurd in the front yard of a suburban house.

When used formally, stone is classic and very elegant. Stone slabs can be cut into square or rectangular flat pieces or sawn for straight architectural edges. Stones can also be used less formally—each one placed uncut in the landscape.

The Japanese rely on the precise placement of stepping-stones in their gardens to conduct movement. The common layout patterns for stepping-stones are:

These patterns are adapted from *Gardens of Japan* by Teiji Itoh

JAPANESE STEPPING-STONE PATTERNS

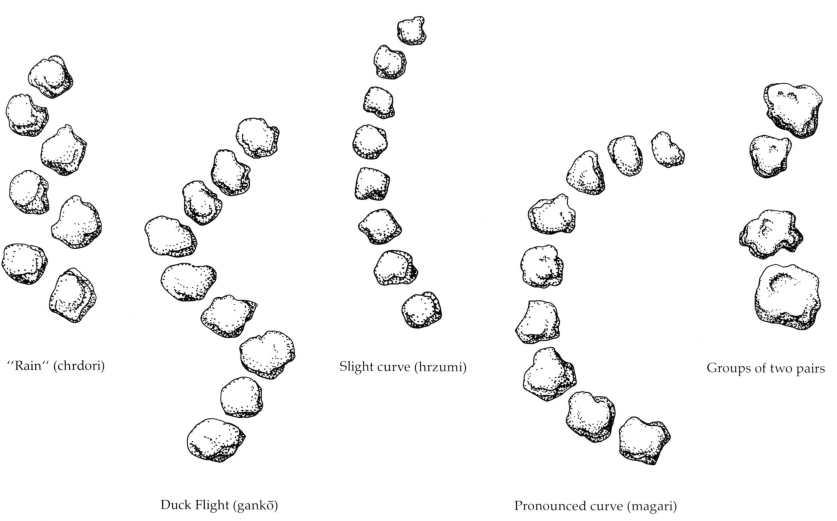

"Rain" (chrdori)

Slight curve (hrzumi)

Groups of two pairs

Duck Flight (gankō)

Pronounced curve (magari)

Flowers at Dusk (rakka)

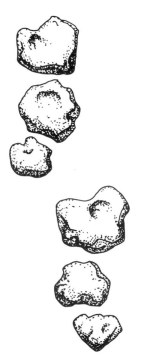

Groups of three pairs

PLANTS FOR BETWEEN STEPPING-STONES ALONG PATHS

Alyssum
Anchust
Androsace (rock jasmine)
Arabis (rock cress)
Arenaria (sand wort)
Armeria (thrift, orscapink)
Aubrieta deltoidea
Aurinia saxatilis
Campanula (the low varieties)
Dianthus (miniature)
Gazania (African daisy)

Gypsophila repens (baby's breath)
Iberis (candytuft)
Lewisia
Lobilia
Malcolmia (virginia stock)
Myosotis (forget-me-nots)
Oxalis adenophylla and *O.hirta*
Phlox (short varieties)
Saxifrage
Sedum
Thumus

Stepping-stones can be interplanted with creeping thyme, chamomile, or mint to emit an herbal fragrance when trod upon. If slabs of stone, wood, or cement at least 12 inches (30 centimeters) thick are available, they can be set 8 to 9 inches (20 to 23 centimeters) above the soil level. The spaces in between can then be planted with dwarf flowering annuals and perennials that form low tufts of blooms, creeping carpets of scented foliage, and airy flowers. Plants suitable for rock and alpine gardens do quite well among stepping-stone crevices. The path can be transformed into a flowering tapestry of blended colors and textures, with raised stepping-stones.

WATER

"Fountains and waters are the soul of a garden; they make their chief ornament and enliven and revive them. How often it is that a garden, beautiful though it be, will seem sad and dreary and lacking in one of its most gracious features, if it has no water," wrote Pierre Husson in his book *La Theorie et la Pratique du Jardinage,* in 1711.

Pierre Husson's observations are just as valid today as they were three hundred years ago. Fountains are most effective when the water is caught in shallow, light-colored basins, where light adds sparkle and bounce. Basins made of glazed or tinted ceramic or cement, colored stone, or hand-painted tile with mosaic patterns will add color to the water. If you are unsure of what colors or trim to use, remember simplicity is best.

In a stream or waterfall use the biggest local stones (usually transported with a forklift) that will fit with the scale of the water feature and garden space. When the rocks used are indigenous to the landscape and have been selected and placed with care, the waterfall will be far more convincing. It is best to place the water source above eye level, and the waterfall should start with a slight downhill stream. Waterfalls can be designed with recirculating pumps so that the water flows into a lower pool for swimming or reflection (usually passing through a filter first). Moss, ferns, grasses, and alpine plants can be naturalized in the rock crevices.

For centuries, rills and rivulets have been used to add sound, movement, and coolness, and to introduce geometric patterns in an otherwise hot, arid landscape. They may be only three to eight inches (eight to twenty centimeters) in width and depth and constructed from flat stone, cement, or tile. Rills often run down staircases, form mini moats, or divide a terrace. Since most people are drawn to visually follow a stream, this design feature is very successful in conducting movement in the landscape.

An English teak bench (facing page, above left) makes a fine accent in this formal water garden, featuring a waterlily pool and bronze herons once used in French estates to deter real herons from stealing fish. Facing page, below left: *Much of the appeal of water in a garden results from the splashing sounds coming from a waterfall and overflows.* Facing page, left: *A naturally designed pool edged with boulders and bordered with Livingstone daisies is interplanted with iris.*

Bridges can serve both a functional and decorative purpose. Right: *A wooden footbridge, strong enough to support a lawn tractor, spans a stream.* Below: *A wooden bridge with a garden bench built into one side, allows visitors to pause and admire a lake vista.*

BRIDGES

Besides functioning as a crossing, a bridge can provide a focal point or a special vantage point in a landscape. Bridge designs can have beautiful forms. For example, moon bridges form a complete circle when reflected into water. It is important, however, that the bridge be in scale and harmony with the water.

Bridges also provide opportunities to design special features for photographers and painters. Claude Monet built his famous footbridge over the waterlily pond to add interest to the scene for a painting. The bridge was inspired from one of his Japanese woodblocks. Later, he added the wisteria-covered arbor for even greater appeal.

PATTERNS

Patterns are used in a landscape either to make strong, dominant statements or to add subtle detail.

STRONG PATTERNS IN THE LANDSCAPE:

Parterres

Embroidery patterns laid out in boxwood like those at Versailles.

Knot Gardens

Various-colored foliages, usually herbs, planted and trimmed into interlocking curves or geometric shapes.

Pebble Gardens

Courtyards of carefully selected pebbles of various colors and sizes placed in mosaic-type patterns.

Walkways

Laid out with an overall shape that creates a pattern in the landscape.

Clipped dwarf hedges (above) form diamond-shaped flower beds filled with wax begonias called "parterres". Right: A pair of strong wooden slabs are placed side-by-side to create a simple oriental-style "zig-zag" bridge. Facing page, above: Liriope—a grass-like groundcover—creates a beautifully textured appearance on a slope where lawn grass would be less appealing. Facing page, below: Broken flagstone has been artistically arranged to make a path that looks more dramatic after a rainfall makes it glisten.

Patios and Terraces

Constructed from various paving materials to create patterns of contrasting lines and colors.

STRONG PATTERN SHAPES:

Zig-zag lines

Will strongly emphasize movement and direction.

Spiral and concentric lines

Usually confine the space and create a static feeling.

Curvilinear lines

Usually give a restful, leisurely quality to the landscape.

Straight lines

Tend to be formal and direct visually; the eye looks quickly down a straight line (such as a straight walk or *allée*).

Broken lines

Creates the illusion of a longer length, because the eye pauses to focus on the breaks. A straight walk can be interrupted visually with statues, pots, trees, arches, etc.

SUBTLE PATTERNS IN THE LANDSCAPE:

Annuals/perennials

Use constrasting textures and colors in groups next to one another in a bed or border.

Hedges and shrubs

Sheared into various shapes that work together to create line, movement, and an overall pattern.

Trees

Planted formally in lines or groves or individually—the trunk, limbs, and leaves create shadow patterns and silhouettes.

Grasses

A lawn can be left unmowed or rough-mowed in specific shapes to create a pattern that contrasts with the very short lawn. Ornamental grasses can be planted in drifts of subdued patterns.

The circular design of this herb garden (left) is accentuated by a centerpiece in the form of an English lead hare. A stepping stone path (right) gracefully curves from one garden area to another. This flagstone path (facing page, far right) curves, adding depth to this garden.

CURVES

Curves soften a landscape and give it a calm, leisurely, romantic feeling. They are used in designing panels of lawn, rounded terraces, archways, pools, hedges, gates, rounded shrubs, and trees or to lay out walks, paths, flower beds, and borders. Look for curves in the architecture of the house and in the surrounding landscape—rolling hills, dunes, or trees. By repeating curves, a rhythm occurs. Three types of curves that are helpful to landscape designers are:

CIRCULAR CURVES

Circular curves are the perfectly round circles that are drawn with a compass. These curves can be interrupted with a straight line called a tangent. Pools, lawns, terraces, and special plantings of herbs, roses, bulbs, and annuals are pleasing when laid out in circular curves.

COMPOUND CURVES

Compound curves are made up of two or more curves of different sizes, united at the edges. For example, a slice of a small tart and a slice of a large piece of pie matched neatly at the edges form a compound curve—more of an oval or bell shape than a circle. When the radius continually gets shorter it becomes a spiral like a nautilus shell. In landscapes, compound curves are most useful in arches, driveways, lawns, and edges.

REVERSE CURVES

These occur when two or more curves going in opposite directions are joined to-

gether like an "S" or hairpin. To avoid a contrived, "wiggly effect" place a long or short line between the curves to give the eye a moment to rest. Reverse curves make lovely flower beds, pathways, and stepping-stone patterns.

Lay out curves in the garden by using stakes and string like a compass to make circular curves or as a tangent to establish straight lines. Reverse curves can be roughly laid out with flexible garden hoses or heavy ropes or temporarily marked with bonemeal or gypsum poured evenly from a watering can with a narrow nozzle.

chapter nine

ESTABLISHING BOUNDARIES

Mᴏꜱᴛ

landscaped properties have two types of

boundaries—the boundaries to the prop-

erty itself and the boundaries to garden

spaces within the property. Boundaries can

be highly visual—marked by a line of trees,

a tall hedge, or a stout wall—or they can be

unobtrusive, blending in with the surround-

ings so successfully that there is no appar-

ent division between the property and the

landscape beyond.

Several considerations are important when deciding how to treat boundaries. Foremost is whether the property needs a definite barrier to ensure privacy and security. If it *is* necessary to protect the property against intruders, then walls and fences may be necessary. However, the forbidding aspect of a wall or fence can often be tempered by planting a line of trees or shrubs in front of it, by covering the wall with vines, or by establishing an informal screen (such as a grove of bamboo) on one or both sides. Stout wooden fences and high chain-link fences can be disguised with similar plantings. It is possible to use a chain-link fence as a "support" for imaginative hedge plantings. For example, a honeysuckle or rose hedge planted alone may not be a dense enough boundary to provide good security from persistent trespassers, but with a chain-link fence hidden in the middle it becomes a formidable barrier. Chain-link fences are available with a black or green vinyl covering, which blends into the landscape.

Above: *This terrace takes full advantage of the view of the water to expand the apparent size of the garden.* Left: *A brick wall forms a solid boundary while providing a very attractive garden foil.* Right: *Dense hedges, such as this burning bush, form an impenetrable boundary between properties.*

BORROWED LANDSCAPES

Some of the most successful garden landscapes seem deceptively large, because their vistas extend beyond the garden's boundaries. The Japanese are particularly adept at designing boundaries to bring a "borrowed" landscape—bamboo-clad hillsides or rugged mountain peaks—into view. In many instances, a city garden is completely surrounded by houses, but a nearby high hill or mountain may extend above and beyond the city environs. A landscape designer will use a low hedge to screen out rooftops and bring into focus the unspoiled mountaintop, creating the illusion that the city garden is surrounded by spectacular wilderness.

without obstructing the view. They also deter stray animals—particularly dogs and deer—from trespassing. When installing a ha-ha on level ground, it is necessary to dig a trench about 6 feet (1.8 meters) wide with a steep slope up to the sunken stone wall. A flight of steps with a gate at the top will allow people to negotiate the ha-ha, while keeping animals out. George Washington and Thomas Jefferson both used ha-has in their private landscapes.

MOATS

In ancient times many fortified manor houses used moats for protection. Today, in Europe, many historic houses have moats or even double moats filled with lazy goldfish and decorated with water-loving

BERMS

A berm is a raised mound of soil covered with grass, shrubs, trees, or other vegetation. It is an excellent device for screening out an eyesore—such as a busy highway—without building anything so solid as a wall or fence. Berms make good boundaries because they have such a comfortable, natural appearance.

HA-HAS

A ha-ha is a solid stone wall set into a slope so that it is invisible from above, but a formidable obstacle when approached from below. Ha-has were extremely popular in colonial days, since their principal purpose was to keep cattle and horses from encroaching on the house. Today, ha-has are used to create a decorative barrier plants such as waterlilies. Moats make good protective boundaries at the edge of a property if the ground is flat and the owner wants to be able to see beyond them to a pastoral or park-like landscape. Closer to the house itself, moats can be useful design features. A theme garden or a guest cottage, for example, might feature a moat not only for privacy, but also to define the space.

Moats do not need to completely encircle a space to be an effective boundary. A partial moat can extend in an L shape; also, a simple canal or a rectangular reflecting pool can help form a boundary along one side. Features such as these work especially well in romantic gardens since the surface of the water—and the margins— can be richly planted with aquatic and bog-loving plants.

F acing page, above:

Banked terraces overflowing with flowering annuals

create a boundary between a residence and a parking

area. Left: *This ha-ha at the historic home of 18th*

century botanist, John Bartram, in Philadelphia, keeps

stray animals away without restricting the view.

Above: *This suburban house features a dry moat with a*

Japanese-style footbridge leading to the front door.

A *billowing boxwood hedge* **(above)** *effectively divides a flagstone sitting area from a rectangular lawn bounded by perennial borders.* **Above right:** *This close-up of a perennial border shows a brick wall creating an enclosure within the garden's outer boundaries. The wooden rail fence beyond the wall hides a vegetable garden.* **Right:** *Dry walls are good boundaries to consider where a steep change in elevation occurs. Here, creeping phlox and other drought-resistant perennials are used to decorate the wall.*

BOUNDARIES BETWEEN FUNCTIONAL AREAS

These boundaries can be much more imaginative than property boundaries. Unless the objective is to create garden rooms (see page 32)—when screens and hedges are desirable—quite often the boundary of a functional space is marked by a simple change of paving material. For example, a barbecue area might be paved with flagstone; a change to brick paving might denote a patio area surrounding a swimming pool; a change to redwood might mark a deck for lounging; and another change to smooth white pebbles might designate a sunbathing area.

Boundaries for functional spaces can also be marked by a change of elevation—a sitting area raised above a slope by means of a terrace; a deck for relaxation raised above a lawn for children's play.

To separate play and relaxation spaces from display gardens, low hedges and walls are useful. An herb garden may need to be completely enclosed by a picket fence to keep out pets and neighborhood wildlife. If the herb garden merely needs defining for ornamental effect, a low hedge of boxwood, lavender, myrtle, or barberry may be preferred.

*I*n this design by the Brickman Group, the rear of a suburban house uses changes in elevation and paving materials to establish boundaries from one garden space to another. Above: A colorful perennial border serves as a boundary for an elliptical lawn. The red flowering plants in the foreground are bergamot.

TRANSITIONS

Where a home landscape has special spaces—such as an orchard at the back of the house, an oriental garden to one side, an herb garden on another side, and a perennial garden up front, it is important to consider transitions. Often a transition is created simply by a gate, but there are many other creative choices—an archway cut into a high hemlock hedge, a pleached "tunnel" made from pliable branches woven over a wire frame (hornbeam and beech work well). Steps, stepping-stones, changes in a path's color (from beige gravel to white oyster shells), are also effective devices to create transitions from one functional space to another.

Where a gate is used as a transition, consider whether you want the gate to be solid, so the area beyond is a total surprise when entered, or whether you want visitors to see through the gate—in which case trelliswork or grillwork should be considered. A gate you can see through makes the space beyond more inviting, while a solid gate or door has the ability to deter entry. For an even greater feeling of freedom than a "see-through" gate, consider an archway without a gate. People are drawn to archways, eager to investigate the space beyond.

*T*his wrought-iron gate *(above) serves as an effective transition from a formal garden to an informal woodland garden by allowing the visitor to see beyond the wall boundary and anticipate a change of scenery.* Right: *An arbor provides the transition from one garden space to another. This arbor provides entrance to an herb garden, with matching arbor leading into a woodland garden.*

Above left: *The severe lines of a stone wall are softened by a row of fragrant lilacs which stretch over the top. Above: Bridges spanning a steam form natural boundaries. Even if a stream divides different properties, neighbors often agree to share a bridge as a decorative feature.*

PROMINENT BOUNDARIES

These devices can screen out eyesores, provide security, and establish a sense of privacy.

> **Fences** (wood or metal)
> **Hedges** (deciduous or evergreen)
> **Walls** (brick or stone)
> **Windbreaks** (trees or tall shrubs)

UNOBTRUSIVE BOUNDARIES

These devices help a property blend in with its surroundings. They can be used alone or in combination with the list above for extra security and protection.

> **Balustrade** (also railings)
> **Berms** (mounds)
> **Brambles** (blackberry, raspberry, wild roses)
> **Changes in Elevation** (terraces, decks, sunken gardens)
> **Changes in Paving Materials** (flagstone, brick, gravel, oyster shells, cement, wood)
> **Curbs** (edging of cement, brick, benderboard, cobblestones, railroad ties)
> **Groves** (bamboo, dogwoods, pines)
> **Ha-ha** (also ravines and dry stream beds)
> **Moats** (also streams and canals)
> **Psychological Boundary** (like the low rail along a winding road, it will not physically keep a car from going over but it serves as a reminder)
> **Visual Boundary** (stops the eye at a chosen focal point without having to construct an actual barrier)

appendix i

CREATING A BLUEPRINT

There are several approaches to making a blueprint of your garden. The most important reason to have working drawings is to have a clear point of reference, a road map of how the landscape is now and how it is planned to be. Blueprints are an invaluable means of communicating the designer's ideas. The process of making a landscape plan is full of valuable lessons. Keep the plan simple, clear, and neat. Don't be concerned with fancy graphics but do be as accurate as possible with actual measurements and reduced scale. Consistency of measurements is essential. Use a 25-foot (7.6-meter) measuring tape and a 100-foot (30.5-meter) cloth tape for outdoors; take careful notes and measure from several key points of reference, such as the corner of the house, a utility pole, or a mature tree.

There are two types of information to gather: *existing conditions* of the landscape, which include the lot size, where the house and other major features sit, and the planned *functions and effects* to be created with the final design.

EXISTING CONDITIONS

1) Establish property lines and layout. Your property title or deed should have these dimensions, or check city or county records for lot sizes.

2) House layout on property. The architect's plan will help, but field measurements will give you a good idea.

3) Note size and location of major features: detached garage, gazebo, patios, pool, mature hedges, and trees.

4) Note where water, gas, and sewer lines are. IMPORTANT if major building, grading, or digging is planned. Many building and irrigation contractors use a metal detector to find old unknown lines.

5) Note the sun's movement and prevailing winds throughout the day and in different seasons: Which areas get the most sun? Where are the shaded corners and filtered light?

FUNCTIONS AND EFFECTS

1) Who will use the garden? How will they use it? List the activities that will be done—dining on a patio, cut flower growing, sunbathing, children's play area, dog kennel and run, etc.

2) List what design features are desired, such as a swimming pool, landscaped driveway, fence for privacy, perennial flower borders, greenhouse, shade areas, improved walkways and entryways, etc.

3) Assess your garden's basic attributes. List existing features you intend to preserve: a view, mature trees, old wisteria, a brick wall, etc.

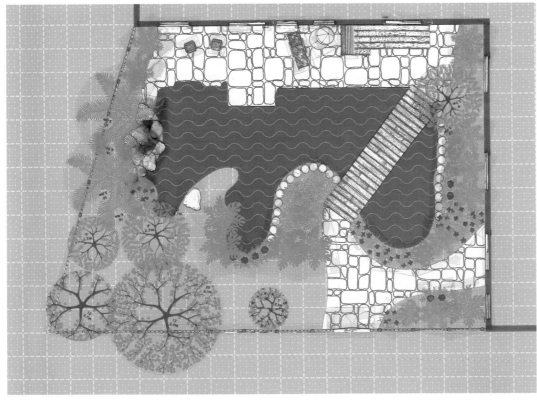

*T*his small courtyard garden features Oriental elements. A Chinese-style gate (top left) leads visitors along a flagstone path, past a tall Japanese stone lantern, over a wooden footbridge to an observation deck that provides a good view of a goldfish pond. A squat stone lantern (above) is an important feature of this garden. Shown in the blueprint at left is a rocky cliff and waterfall that butt against a garage wall. This and other blueprints on the following pages were made from a Planaflex design kit using pressure-sensitive transfers.

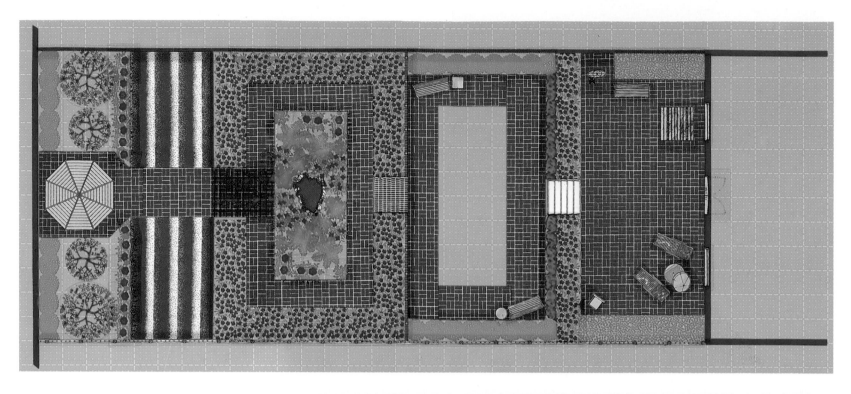

A long, narrow city
backyard (above) *features garden spaces on three levels,
with a gazebo as a focal point. The first garden level is a
brick patio descending to a formal garden* (right). *A
divider of arches separates this formal area from a more
informal garden space including a sundial garden*
(facing page, above) *and an herb garden with a bird
bath* (facing page, below), *laid out in a cartwheel
design.*

4) Features to remove or change: enlarge terrace; remove old shed; convert detached garage to charming garden house; prune major trees; replace tumbling arbor.

5) Analyze what appeals to you. Is it clear, orderly straight lines and neat walkways, a profusion of flowers like an English cottage garden, the simplicity of water and rocks and greenness like the Japanese gardens, the adherence to a strict color code, a tropical feeling, a romantic or European feeling, a postmodern style, or a natural woodland feeling?

What are your favorite plants? Collect photos of gardens you like. Make "recipe" cards of plant combinations you like. This will aid you in your observation of other gardens and help you to remember color schemes, texture, and moods you enjoyed somewhere.

6) Realities:

Time—How much maintenance time can you afford?

Budget—For installation, special projects, plant materials, improvements, labor? Per month? Per year? Over the next five years?

Water—Do you have a limited water supply? How is your water pressure? Are there droughts in your area? (If yes, consider drought-tolerant landscaping, using native plants and drip irrigation.) What is the quality of your water? Will you have to irrigate in the dry season? If so, what will be your method—by hose, irrigation system, manual or on a timer, drip or overhead sprinklers (good to cover distance but can spread rust and mildew and destroy flowers)?

Animal problems—Deer, gophers, dogs, muskrats (disaster for pond edges and water lilies)

Soil test—pH and quality; does it require amendments because it is too sandy or has a clay base?

Preparation Time—proper preparation of the site contributes to a garden's success, but can be quite costly. It can include: soil improvement, grading and leveling, drainage improvement, irrigation system installation (less expensive and less obtrusive if done before major plantings), as well as construction of paths, walkways, terraces, fences, walls, and lighting systems.

A design kit called *PLANAFLEX Putting Plans on Paper* helps to draft and design a home landscape. Using the vinyl gridboard and dozens of vinyl graphic symbols, one can lay out the house, cut a swimming pool to scale, and place various paving surfaces for drives, decks, and steps. Plant materials include deciduous and evergreen trees, shrubs, ground covers, hedges, vines, and flowers. Even stones, railroad ties, spotlights, fences, sprinkler systems, and outdoor furniture are provided. The design manual has good, clear ideas that are easy to follow. It is a great advantage to be able to experiment with the placement of various landscape elements. The final scheme can be photocopied or traced, and then blueprints can be made from the tracings for working plans.

to be able to experiment with the placement of various landscape elements. The final scheme can be photocopied or traced, and then blueprints can be made from the tracings for working plans.

One method that works well for both the professional and the beginner is to draw an "as is" elevation, and then superimpose alternative design ideas. Here's how: Start with your entrance; with black and white or color print film (not slides) take several photos of your house:

1) The front door with entrance landing
2) The house including the roof line
3) The front including the driveway, flower beds, foundation plantings, paths, fences, or gates.

When you look into the camera, frame a picture of your house, and make sure each photo tells you some specific information. Try to take *front-on* photos, rather than angle shots. (Angle shots tend to get more subject into a photo, but for this purpose there is too much distortion.)

Study photographs carefully. Choose the pictures that tell clear information about the landscape. Bring these photos to a print shop with photocopiers that *enlarge* (check the phone book). Get your snapshots enlarged to a 8½ x 11 inch (22 x 28 centimeters) size.

Buy a roll of tracing paper at an office supply store. Have sharp pencils, a black felt-tipped pen, a gum eraser, a good ruler, and some masking tape.

If you happen to have a light table, use it. If not, a glass table can be used by putting a lamp beneath it, or you can use a bright light and press hard. If you have difficulty seeing some details, tape the photocopy and tracing paper to a window with sunlight coming through. Once you put down the enlargement with your tracing paper over it, don't move it—tape it in place.

Now carefully trace the outline of your house, the door, the eves, the existing steps, path, or flower beds. Draw in all the architectural features.

Place a second layer of tracing paper over the first; tape it down so it doesn't move, and draw in your existing shrubs, trees, hedges, flower borders, foundation plants, etc. This is your "composite drawing" of how the entrance looks now. Study it objectively. Are there overgrown shrubs covering the windows or juniper taking over the path? Are the plantings in proportion to the size and style of your house? Would a curving path be more attractive than a straight one dividing the property?

Experiment with your design ideas on a third sheet of tracing paper placed on top of the xerox. Draw in the new, enlarged flower beds or take out the overgrown shrubs. Visualize the difference it will make.

If you have a new, unplanted site, overlays of tracing paper will allow you to try drawing different shapes to get an idea of forms and proportion. Your house may have a special architectural feature you want to bring out, such as a round window, some detailed trim, a porch, etc. You may have some aspects of your

house you want to screen (the garbage area, side yard, etc.) or a corner you'd like to soften with a climbing rose, wisteria, or other vine. It might be a period house (Victorian, Colonial, Cape Cod, Early American), which may inspire you to install a "period" garden. Look in books and magazines about gardens and design to get different approaches to solve a problem. Develop a critical, observant eye and don't be afraid to throw out ideas—bad ones and good ones—if they aren't appropriate to your home or lifestyle.

Your finished traced drawing can be cleaned up and made into a blueprint.

When designing planting areas, many landscape designers prefer to work directly on site. Garden hoses are employed to lay curved walks and beds; flour and bonemeal is sprinkled to indicate where drifts of bulbs or groupings of annuals will be planted. With careful measurements of given points, these "free-hand" site designs can also be graphed on paper. It is essential to a successful landscape plan for the designer to work on site as well as at the drafting table.

*T*his rectangular plot is typical of both city and suburban gardens. Here, the owner has divided the rectangle into two parts—a vegetable garden featuring raised beds in the lower half (facing page, left) and a flower garden in the upper half, visible from the house (right). A flagstone sitting area leads off from a glass-enclosed porch (far right). The two spaces are connected by an arbor and divided by a hedge. The potted banana stays outdoors in summer and is moved into the heated porch area during winter.

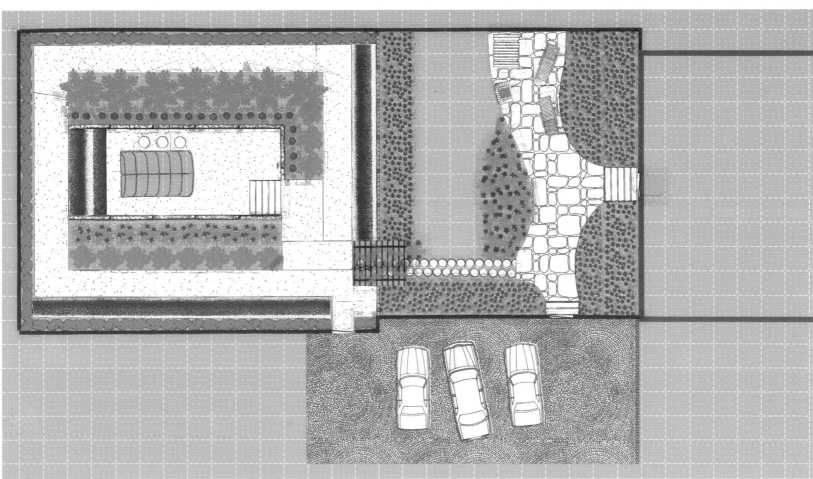

13 GARDEN ELEMENTS THAT ADD VALUE TO YOUR HOME

1) A View—framed by plantings; a vista created by the garden design
2) Mature Trees—treasure any you may have
3) Established Hedges—provide privacy and screen; not the type that are overgrown and block out light and views
4) Flowering shrubs, trees, and hedges
5) Perennial flower beds
6) Landscaped driveways
7) Privacy from street—established attractively by hedges, fence, or wall
8) Terraces, brick or wooden decking—for outdoor entertaining/eating
9) Charm—personality in a garden
10) Garden accents (in good condition and taste)—gazebos, arches, arbors, bridges
11) Water feature—a small pond, waterfall, fountain
12) Low maintenance aspects—automatic irrigation, plant choice, and overall design
13) Attractive toolshed/storage area/service areas

The blueprint below shows elements that create an illusion of greater distance. A lawn is made progressively narrower by means of flower and shrub borders (facing page, top far right), edged in brick. The lawn vista also features dot-dash progression of two rectangular flower beds and a circular bed (facing page, top right), leading the eye to a trompe l'oeil archway of trellis work providing a focus from the neighboring building (facing page, bottom, far right). A high brick wall screens the garden from a busy street, its large expanse of brick softened by flowering vines (facing page, bottom right).

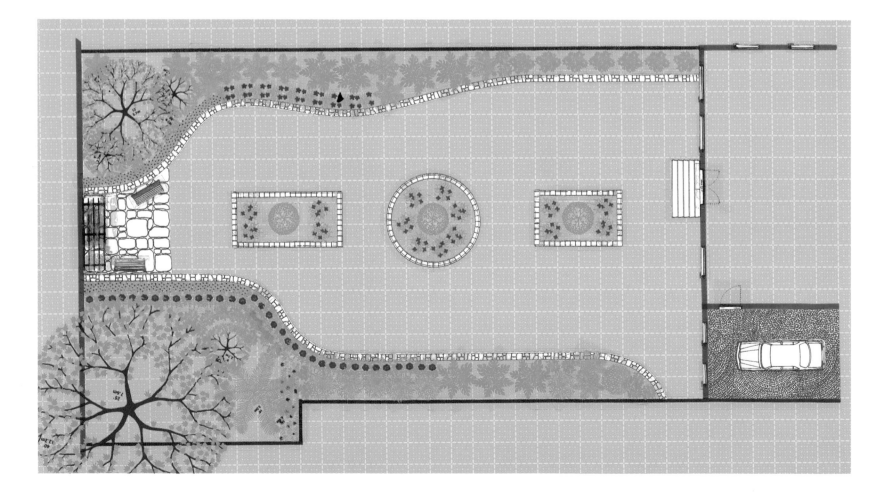

appendix ii

SOURCES, USEFUL ADDRESSES, AND DESIGNERS

CONSERVATORIES/ GREENHOUSES

Amdega Centre
160 Friendship Road
Cranbury, NJ 08512
(201) 329-0999
Conservatories hand-crafted in England

Everlite Aluminum Greenhouses, Inc.
P.O. Box 11087
Cleveland, OH 44111
Prefabricated for quick assembly

Janco Greenhouses
Dept. H-1, 9390 Davis Avenue
Laurel, MD 20707
(301) 498-5700

Machin Designs (USA) Inc.
652 Glenbrook Road
Stamford, CT 06906
(203) 348-5319
Conceived in the Victoria Romantic
Tradition, built in England

Texas Greenhouse Company
2713 St. Louis Avenue
Ft. Worth, TX 76110
(817) 926-5447

GAZEBOS

Jim Dalton Garden House Co.
7260-68 Oakley Street
Philadelphia, PA 19111
(215) 342-9804
Western Red Cedar in the Finest
Woodworking Tradition

Vintage Gazebos
Dept. 367, 513 S. Adams
Fredericksburg, TX 78624
(512) 997-9513

Vixen Hill
Dept. GD, R.D. 2
Phoenixville, PA 19460
(215) 827-7972
Traditional designs

LIGHTING FOR THE GARDEN

Genie House
Handcrafted Lighting Fixtures
P.O. Box 2478
Vincentown, NJ 08088
(609) 654-8303

Greenlee Landscape Lighting
Dallas, TX
(214) 484-1133

Hanover Lantern
Division of Hoffman Products, Inc.
470 High Street
Hanover, PA 17331

Idaho Wood
P.O. Box 488
Sandpoint, KS 83864
Wood lighting fixtures

Loran Incorporated
1705 East Colton Avenue
Redlands, CA 92373

Luminae, Jan Lennox Moyer
6225 Chelton Drive
Piedmont, CA 94611
(415) 482-1862
lighting consultants and designers

Philip Hawk & Company
159 East College Avenue
Pleasant Gap, PA 16823
(814) 355-7177
stone lanterns

John Watson Landscape Illumination
Nationwide
(214) 630-7751

Woodform
9705 N.E. Colfax Street
Portland, OR 97220
(503) 253-9626
toll free (800) 624-5091
redwood light fixtures

PLANT AND HORTICULTURAL SOCIETIES

American Bamboo Society,
Northern California Chapter
666 Wagnon Road
Sebastopol, CA 95472

American Begonia Society
ABS-PH, Box 1129
Encinitas, CA 92024

The American Fuchsia Society
Dept. P, County Fair Building
9th Avenue & Lincoln Way
San Francisco, CA 94122

American Iris Society
1914 Napa Street
Berkeley, CA 94707

American Ivy Society
P.O. Box 520
West Carrollton, OH 45449

American Rhododendron Society
14885 SW Sunrise Lane
Tigard, OR 97224

The American Rock Garden Society
Buffy Parker, Secretary
15 Fairmead Road
Darien, CT 06820

American Rose Society,
San Francisco Chapter
68 Fernwood Drive
San Francisco, CA 94127

Bulbous Plant Yearbook
APLS-PH, P.O. Box 150
La Jolla, CA 92038

California Horticultural Society
California Academy of Sciences
Golden Gate Park
San Francisco, CA 94118

California Rare Fruit Growers,
SF Bay Area Chapter
2209 McGee Avenue
Berkeley, CA 94703

Herb Society of America
2 Independence Court
Concord, MA 01742

International Fern Society
P.O. Box 90943
Pasadena, CA 91109-0943

Pacific Horticulture
P.O. Box 485
Berkeley, CA 94701

Scottish Rock Garden Club
Secretary Kirsten Gibb
21 Merchiston Park
Edinburgh EH104PW, Scotland

Texas State Horticultural Society
P.O. Box 10025
College Station, TX 77840

HERBS

Caprilands Herb Farm
Silver Street
Coventry, CT 06238
(203) 742-7244
Plants, seeds, gifts, lectures, display gardens

Fox Hill Farm
440 W. Michigan Ave.
Dept. H41, Box 9
Parma, MI 49269
(517) 531-3179
350 varieties of herbs and scented geraniums

Flower Valley Herbs
Route 2, Box 22
Dixon, IA 52745
(319) 843-3400
Plants, crafts, gifts, workshops

The Herb Cottage
Washington Cathedral
Mt. St. Alban, Washington D.C. 20016
(202) 537-6230
Plants, products, crafts, gifts, herb gardens

Nichols Garden Nursery
1190 N. Pacific Hwy.
Albany, OR 97321
(503) 928-9280
Plants, seeds, products

Taylor's Herb Gardens
1535 Lone Oak Rd.
Vista, CA 92083
Plants and seeds

GARDEN FURNITURE

Backhouse, Inc.
4121 Hillsboro Rd., Suite 301
Nashville, TN 37215

Basta Sole
4901 E. 12th Street
Oakland, CA 94601
(415) 436-8616
Designer market umbrellas

British-American Marketing
   Services, Ltd.
251 Welsh Pool Road
Lionville, PA 19353

Craft House/Colonial Williamsburg
P.O. Box CH, Dept. 2217
Williamsburg, VA 23187
1-800-446-9240
Classical teak

The Chattahoochee Makers Company
1098 Huff Rd., N.W.
Atlanta, GA 30318
(404) 351-7016
Mahogany

Clapper's
Dept. GD1286
1121 Washington St.
West Newton, MA 02165
(617) 244-7900
English teak

Country Casual—CAH
17317 Germantown Road
Germantown, MD 20874-2999
(301) 540-0040
Teak

Dura Art Stone
P.O. Box 666
Fontana, CA 92334
(714) 350-9000
(800) 821-1120
Classic and custom designs

Lister Teak
561 Exton Commons
Exton, PA 19341
1-800-345-TEAK

Lyon-Shaw
Department GD-03
1538 Salisbury Boulevard West
Salisbury, NC 28144

Moquette
Showplace Square West
550 15th Street
San Francisco, CA 94103
(415) 621-5600
Bosh, cast stone furniture, planters, flooring

Park Place
2251 Wisconsin Ave., NW
Washington, D.C. 20007
(202) 342-6294

Reed Bros.
Turner Station
Sebastopol, CA 95472
(707) 795-6261
Hand-carved redwood, indoor/outdoor

Simms & Thayer
205 Oak Street
Pembroke, MA 02359
White, enamel

Shears & Window Garden Court
5 Henry Adams Street
San Francisco, CA 94103
(415) 626-9080
Distinctive garden ornaments & furniture

Summit Furniture Incorporated
P.O. Box S
Carmel, CA
Teak garden furniture

SCULPTURE

Aristides Demetrios
69 Bluxome Street
San Francisco, CA 94107
(415) 788-3461
Wonderful, large, contemporary garden sculpture and fountains, steel and bronze

Shears & Window Garden Court
5 Henry Adams Street
San Francisco, CA 94103
(415) 626-9084
French, English, and Italian antiques and reproduction

Southern Statuary & Stone
3401 5th Ave. So.
Birmingham, AL 35222

GATES, FENCES, SCREENS, AND STAIRS

California Redwood Association
591 Redwood Highway
Mill Valley, CA 94941

Grate Works
Lucia Demetrios
69 Bluxome Street
San Francisco, CA 94107
(415) 788-3461
Sculptural, Matisse-like cut out steel gates
and furniture, natural and in colors

Moultrie Manufacturing Company
P.O. Drawer 1179, Dept. GI1
Moultrie, GA 31776-1179
1-800-841-8674
Old South cast aluminum fences and gates

Sloan Miyasato
2 Henry Adams Street #207
San Francisco, CA 94103
(415) 431-1465
Japanese screens, lanterns, teahouses

Steptoe & Wife Antiques Ltd.
322 Geary Avenue
Toronto, Ontario, Canada M6H 2C7
(416) 530-4200
Victorian design cast iron stairs, handrails

WATER GARDEN SUPPLIERS/ DESIGNERS

Designs for Outdoor Living
Box 953
Los Altos, CA 94022
(415) 941-9070
Ceramic and bamboo fountains, water
features, rock formations

Di Giacomo
612 South Duggan Avenue
Azusa, CA 91702-5138
(818) 334-8211

Lilypons Water Gardens
2900 Design Road
P.O. Box 10
Lilypons, MD 21717-0010
(301) 874-5133

Potomac Waterworks
2451 Potomac Street
Oakland, CA 94602
(415) 482-1007
Paul Cowley, ASLA
Consultants/Designers
Water Gardens and Fish Pond Systems

Slocum Water Gardens
Dept. GD1186
1101 Cypress Gardens Rd.
Winter Haven, FL 33880

Van Ness Water Gardens
2460 North Euclid
Upland, CA 91786
(714) 982-2425

The Water Designers
96 Museum Way
San Francisco, CA 94114
(415) 864-1646

Waterford Gardens
74 East Allendale Road
Saddle River, NJ 07458
(201) 327-0721

PLANTERS

Foster Kevill
15102 Weststate Street
Westminster, CA 92683
(714) 894-2013
Fiberglass and wood

Mrs. McGregor's Teak Garden Boxes
4801-H First St. N.
Arlington, VA 22203
(703) 528-8773

Norstad Pottery
253 S. 25th Street
Richmond, CA 94804
(415) 620-0200
Stoneware planters for inside and outside

Sue Fisher King
3075 Sacramento Street
San Francisco, CA 94115
(415) 922-7276
Italian garden terra cotta

UNIQUE TOOLS, BOOKS, AND GIFTS FOR THE GARDENER

Bell's Book Store
536 Emerson Street
Palo Alto, CA 94301
Specializing in garden books

Eric N. Cogswell
129 Baker Street
San Francisco, CA 94117

The Gardener
1805 Fourth Street
Berkeley, CA 94710

Gardener's Eden
P.O. Box 7307
San Francisco, CA 94120
(415) 428-9292

Jersey Village Gardener, Inc.
P.O. Box 40526, Dept. F1
Houston, TX 77240
(713) 466-3123

David Kay Garden & Gift
    Catalogue, Inc.
26055-D Emery Road
Cleveland, OH 44128
(800) 621-5199

The Kinsman Company
River Road (Dept. 451)
Point Pleasant, PA 18950
(215) 297-5613
Arbors, arches, tools

Lyons Ltd., Antique Prints
2700 Hyde Street
San Francisco, CA 94109
Botanic prints

Nampara Gardens
2004 Gold Course Road
Bayside, CA 95524
(707) 822-5744
Redwood bridges, lanterns, screens

The Plow and Hearth
560 Main Street
Madison, VA 22727

Smith & Hawken
25 Corte Madera
Mill Valley, CA 94941

Urban Farmer Store
2121 Taraval Street
San Francisco, CA 94116
Irrigation and drip systems

TROPICAL AND EXOTIC PLANTS

Bamboo Sorcery
666 Wagon Road
Sebastopol, CA 95472
(707) 823-5866
Over 100 species of bamboo.

California Epi Center
Box 1431PH
Vista, CA 92083
All new 1987 "Flowering Jungle Cactus"
catalog $2.

Desert to Jungle
3211 W. Beverly Blvd.
Montebello, CA 90640
(213) 722-3976
Perennials, ornamental grasses, tropicals
& subtropicals, flowering shrubs, palms,
orchids, and succulents.

Endangered Species
P.O. Box 1830
Tustin, CA 92681
130 bamboo, 180 palms, 80 cycads.

Foliage Gardens
Dept. C, 2003 128th Ave. S.E.
Bellevue, WA 98005
(206) 747-2998
Ferns—hardy and exotic. Catalog $1.

Gate to Eden
328 Mason Road
Vista, CA 92084
(619) 726-9203
Plumeria; catalog $1.

Logee's Greenhouse
Dept. PH, 55 North Street
Danielson, CT 06239
Jasmines, begonias, exotic plants.
Catalog $3.

Living Green Plantscape Design
3 Henry Adams St.
San Francisco, CA 94103
(415) 864-2251
Interior and exterior designers with exotics
and subtropicals.

The Plumeria People
P.O. Box 820013
Houston, TX 77282-0014, Attn: Richard
Plumerias and tropicals. New Handbook of
Plumeria Culture $4.95. Catalog $1.

Rainbow Gardens
Box 721-PHS7
La Habra, CA 90633-0721
Tropical cactus; catalog $1.

Rhapis Gardens
P.O. Box 287-0
Gregory, TX 78359
Lady palms; catalog $1.

Rogers Fujikawa Orchids
530 Flood Ave.
San Francisco, CA 94112
(415) 261-7580
Rare orchids, care, and design available.

Singers
17806 Plummer St. PH
Northridge, CA 91325
(818) 993-1903
Unusual plants. Catalog and periodic
newsletters $1.50.

TREES AND SHRUBS

Including Azaleas, Rhododendrons, fruit,
    and citrus trees

Appalachian Garden
Box 82
Waynesboro, PA 17268
2-year-old plants in 4″ pots.

Bernardo Beach Native Plant Farm
Star Route 7, Box 145
Veguita, NM 87062
Large selection of drought-tolerant native
trees and shrubs. Send four First Class
stamps for list.

Bovees Nursery
1737 Southwest Coronado
Portland, OR 97219
Rhododendrons, azaleas, and Japanese
trees. Catalog $2.

Camellia Forest
125 Carolina Forest Road
Chapel Hill, NC 27514
Many camellias and Asian trees and
shrubs. Send two First Class stamps for
list.

Carlson's Gardens
Box 305-H
South Salem, NY 10590
(914) 763-5958
Hardy, landscape-size azaleas; catalog $2.

Cascade Forestry Service
Route 1
Cascade, IA 52033
Hardwood and shade trees, five feet and
longer, shipped UPS. Free catalog.

Emlong's
Box H-87
Stevensville, MI 49127
Shrubs with berries to attract birds.
Free catalog.

Forestfarm
990 Tetherow Road
Williams, OR 97544
American native plants, unusual
ornamentals and conifers, good to attract
wildlife. Catalog $2.

Four Winds
True Dwarf Citrus Growers
42186 Palm Ave.
Mission San Jose Dist.
Fremont, CA 94539
(415) 656-2591

Foxborough Nursery
3611 Miller Road
Street, MD 21154
Dwarf conifers, many cultivars of Japanese
maple, European beech, and American
hemlock. Catalog $1.

Girard Nurseries
P.O. Box 428
Geneva, OH 44041
Azaleas, Rhododendrons, and broadleaf
evergreens. Free catalog.

Gossler Farms Nursery
1200 Weaver Road
Springfield, OR 97478
(503) 746-3922
Catalog $1.

Greer Gardens
1280 Goodpasture Island Road
Eugene, OR 97401
Rhododendrons, azaleas, ornamental
trees, and flowering shrubs. Catalog $2.

Kelly Brothers Nurseries
Dansville, NY 14437
Native shrubs, fruit trees, and tree wisteria.
Free catalog.

Henry Leuthardt
Dept. 666H
East Moriches, NY 11940
Dwarf fruit trees. Free catalog.

Louisiana Nursery
Route 7, Box 43
Opelousas, LA 70570
325 different magnolia, bamboo,
ornamental trees and shrubs, succulents
and cacti. Catalog $3.50.

Miller Nurseries
Canandaigua, NY 14424
Fruit trees and 'sunburst' locust.
Free catalog.

North Coast Rhododendron Nursery
P.O. Box 308
Bodega, CA 94922
Rhododendrons for mild climates.
Catalog $1.

Pacific Tree Farms
4301 Lynwood Drive
Chula Vista, CA 92010
(619) 422-2400
New and rare plants and trees.
Catalog $1.50.

Sonoma Horticultural Nursery
3970 Azalea Ave.
Sebastopol, CA 95472
(707) 823-6832
Species rhododendrons, hybrid
rhododendrons, exbury azaleas,
evergreen azaleas.

Vireya Specialties Nursery
Dept. P, 2701 Malcolm Ave.
Los Angeles, CA 90064
Rhododendrons; free catalog.

Waynesboro Nurseries
Route 664, Box 987
Waynesboro, VA 22980
Fruit trees, crabapples, double flowering
cherry, pink, red, and white dogwood.
Free catalog.

Weston Nurseries
East Main Street, Route 135, P.O. Box 135
Hopkinton, MA 01748
Trees including double flowering 'apple
blossom', quince, and weeping crabapple.
Free catalog.

Woodlanders
1128 Colleton Avenue
Aiken, SC 29801
Catalog $1.50.

RARE AND UNUSUAL PLANTS, SEEDS, AND BULBS

The Banana Tree
Dept. AH, 715 Northampton St.
Easton, PA 18042
Catalog 50¢.

BioQuest International
P.O. Box 5752
Santa Barbara, CA 93150-5752
Bulbs; catalog $1.

Clyde Robin Seed Co., Inc.
P.O. Box 2366
Castro Valley, CA 94546
Wildflower seeds, annuals, and perennials;
catalog $2.

The Country Garden
Rt. 2H
Crivitz, WI 54114
Flower seed specialists from around the
world. Unusual perennials, annuals, and
wildflower seeds.

International Seed Supplies
Dept. AH, P.O. Box 538
Nowra 2541, N.S.W., Australia

Larner Seeds
Box 407
Bolinas CA 94924
California native plant seed, wildflowers,
perennials, trees, and shrubs. Catalog
75¢.

Lower Daltons Nursery
Richard G. M. Cawthrone
Swanley Village
Swanley Kent BR8 7NU England
Violas, violettas, and viola species.
Assorted seed $5.

Maver Seeds
Rte. 2, Box 265 B
Asheville, NC 28805
(704) 298-4751
Seed; Perennials $2, Tree & Shrub $1.

Moon Mountain (PH)
Box 34
Morrow Bay, CA 93442
Wildflower seed catalog $1.

New Leaf
2456PH Foothill Drive
Vista, CA 92084
(619) 726-9269
Geraniums; catalog $2.

Nichol's Herb and Rare Seeds
1190 W. Pacific
Albany, OR 97321
Unusual varieties of herbs, vegetables,
and flowers suitable for the American
garden.

Novelty Nursery
P.O. Box 382
Novelty, OH 44072
Ferns.

Theodore Payne Foundation
Box PH, 10459 Tuxford Street
Sun Valley, CA 91352
(818) 768-1802
California native plants and seed.

Putney Nursery, Inc.
Box H-71
Putney, VT 05346
Wildflowers, ferns, herbs, and perennials.
Catalog $1.

Robinett Bulb Farm
7349 Healdsburg Ave. #9
Sebastopol, CA 95472
Bulbs and their seeds, California natives,
Mediterraneans, lilies.

Shepherd's Garden Seeds
7389 W. Zayante Rd.
Felton, CA 95018
Catalog $1.

Thompson and Morgan
Box 1308
Jackson, NJ 08527

Vermont Bean Seed Co.
Garden Lane
Bomoseen, VT 05732

Vermont Wildflower Farm
Box H
Charlotte, VT 05445

The Vicarage
Sheffield, New Zealand
Rare and unusual alpine plant seed.
Seed list $1.

IRIS, DAYLILIES, HOSTAS, AND PEONIES

Aitken's Salmon Creek Garden
Dept. P7, 608 NW 119th Street
Vancouver, WA 98685
(206) 573-4472
Irises. Catalog $1.

B&D Lilies
Dept. PH, 330 P Street
Port Townsend, WA 98368
(206) 385-1738
Alstroemeria Ligtu hybrids. Catalog $1.

Bobeleta Gardens, Inc.
15974 Canby Avenue Rte. 5
Fairibault, MN 55021
Northern grown lilies, irises, daffodils.
Catalog $3.

Caprice Farm Nursery
15425P SW Pleasant Hill Rd.
Sherwood, OR 97140
(503) 625-7241
Daylilies, Japanese iris, peonies, and
hosta. Catalog $1.

Chehalem Gardens
P.O. Box 693PH
Newberg, OR 97132
Siberian and spuria iris.

Cooley's Gardens
11553 Silverton Rd. NE
P.O. Box 126P
Silverton, OR 97381
Iris book $2.

Cordon Bleu Farms
Box 2033
San Marcos, CA 92069
Daylilies, Spuria, and Louisiana irises.

Greenwood Nursery
P.O. Box 1610
Goleta, CA 93116
(805) 964-2420
Daylilies; catalog $3.

Iron Gate Gardens
Rte. 3, Box 101
Kings Mountain, NC 28086
Daylilies; catalog $1.50.

Klehm Nursery
Rte. 5, Box 197
South Barrington, IL 60010
Peonies, hostas, daylilies. Catalog $2.

Savory's Greenhouse
5300 Whiting
Edina, MN 55435
Hostas; catalog $1.

Schreiner's Gardens
3625 Quinaby Rd., NE
Salem, OR 97303
Irises; catalog $2.

Gilbert H. Wild & Son, Inc.
H-187 Joplin St.
Sarcoxie, MO 64862
Peonies, daylilies. Catalog $2.

ORNAMENTAL GRASSES

Greenlee Nursery
301 East Franklin Ave.
Pomona, CA 91766
(714) 629-9045
Ornamental grasses, sedges, and rushes.

BLUE PRINTS

PLANAFLEX
A Stanley Tools Company 1987
Division of Stanley Works
New Britain, CT 06050

ALPINE AND ROCK GARDEN PLANTS

Alpine Gardens
15920P SW Oberst Ln.
Sherwood, OR 97140
Sempervivums and sedums.

Oakhill Garden
1960 Cherry Knoll Rd.
Dallas, OR 97338
(503) 623-4612
Sempervivums, sedums, Jovibarba,
Rosularia, Crostachys, Lewisia.

Rich Creek Gardens
1315 66th Ave. NE
Minneapolis, MN 55432
(612) 574-1197
Rock plants, rare alpines, wildflowers.

Siskiyou Rare Plant Nursery
Dept. 72, 2825 Cummings Rd.
Medford, OR 97501
Rock garden and alpine plants.
Catalog $2.

PERENNIALS— UNIQUE AND RARE

Bluestone Perennials
7237 Middle Ridge Rd.
Madison, OH 44057

Canyon Creek Nursery
3527 Dry Creek Road
Oroville, CA 95965
Catalog $1.

Carroll Gardens
444 East Main St.
P.O. Box 310H
Westminster, MD 21157

Forestfarm
990 Tetherpah
Williams, OR 97544
Catalog $2.

Heaths & Heathers
Box 850
Elma, WA 98541
(206) 482-3258
Hardy evergreen heathers.

Holbrook Farm & Nursery
Route 2, Box 223B-7013
Fletcher, NC 28732

Stallings Nursery
910-PH Encinitas Blvd.
Encinitas, CA 92024
Catalog $2.

Trans-Pacific Nursery
29870 Mill Creek Rd.
Sheridan, OR 97378
Free catalog.

Andre Viette
Route 608
Fisherville, VA 22939
(703) 943-2315

Wayside Gardens
Hodges, SC 29695-0001
(800) 845-1124

Western Hills Nursery Rare Plants
16250 Coleman Valley Road
Occidental, CA 95465
(707) 874-3731
Plant list $2.

White Flower Farm
Litchfield, CT 06759
Catalog $5.

Wildwood Farm
10300 Sonoma Hwy.
Kenwood, CA 95452
(707) 833-1161
Hardy perennials, collectibles, California natives.

CANADIAN SOURCES

PLANT AND HORTICULTURAL SOCIETIES

Alberta Horticultural Association
Box 223
Lacombe, Alberta T0C 1S0

Alpine Garden Club of British Columbia
566 Esquimalt Avenue
West Vancouver, British Columbia V7T 1J4

British Columbia Council of Garden Clubs
10595 Dunlop Road
Delta, British Columbia V4C 7G2

Canadian Botanical Association
Department of Botany
University of British Columbia
Vancouver, British Columbia V6T 2B1

Canadian Hobby Greenhouse Association
83-270 Timberbank Boulevard
Agincourt, Ontario M1W 2M1

Canadian Parks/Recreation Association
Association Canadienne des Losirs/Parcs
333 River Road
Vanier, Ontario K1L 8H9

Canadian Wildflower Society
35 Bauer Crescent
Unionville, Ontario L3R 4H3

Fédération des Sociétés d'Horticulture et
   d'Écologie du Québec
1415 rue Jarry est
Montréal, Québec H2E 2Z7

Garden Clubs of Ontario
8 Tanager Avenue
Toronto, Ontario M4G 3R1

Manitoba Horticultural Association
908 Norquay Boulevard
Winnipeg, Manitoba R3C 0P8

New Brunswick Horticultural Society
Department of Agriculture
Horticulture Section
Box 6000
Fredericton, New Brunswick E3B 5H1

Newfoundland Horticultural Society
Box 4326
St. Johns, Newfoundland A1C 6C4

North American Heather Society
1205 Copley Place
R.R. 1
Shawigan Lake, British Columbia
   V0R 2W0

Nova Scotia Association of Garden Clubs
Box 550
Truro, Nova Scotia B2N 5E3

Ontario Horticultural Association
Ontario Ministry of Agriculture and Food
Rural Organizations Service Branch
Box 1030
Guelph, Ontario N1H 6N1

Ontario Rock Garden Society
Box 146
Shelbourne, Ontario L0S 1S0

Prince Edward Island Rural Beautification
   Society
Box 1194
Charlottetown, Prince Edward Island
   C1A 7M8

Rhododendron Society of Canada
R.R.#2
St. George, Ontario N0E 1N0

Royal Botanical Gardens Members
   Association
Box 339
Hamilton, Ontario L8N 3H8

Saskatchewan Horticultural Association
Box 152
Balcarres, Saskatchewan S0G 0C0

La Société d'Animation du Jardin et de
   l'Institut Botaniques
4101 rue Sherbrooke est
Montréal, Québec H1X 2B2

Vancouver Island Rock & Alpine Society
P.O. Box 6507
Station C
Victoria, British Columbia V8P 5Z4

RETAIL NURSERIES

Alberta Nurseries and Seeds, Ltd.
Box 20
Bowden, Alberta T0M 0K0
vegetable and flower seeds, ornamental
and fruit trees

Alberta Nursery Trades Association
10215 176th Street
Edmonton, Alberta T5S 1M1

Alpenglow Gardens
13328 King George Highway
North Surrey, British Columbia V3T 2T6
rare alpines, dwarf conifers, flowering
shrubs

Atlantic Provinces Nursery Trades
   Association
Terra Nova Landscaping
130 Bluewater Road
Bedford, Nova Scotia B4A 1G7

Beaverlodge Nursery Ltd.
Box 127
Beaverlodge, Alberta T0H 0C0
hardy plants suitable for northern gardens

British Columbia Nursery Trade
   Association
Suite #101A-15290 103A Avenue
Surrey, British Columbia V3R 7A2

Canadian Nursery Trades Association
1293 Matheson Boulevard
Mississauga, Ontario L4W 1R1

Canadian Seed Growers Association
237 Argyle Avenue
Box 8455
Ottawa, Ontario K1G 3T1

John Connon Nurseries
Waterdown, Ontario L0R 2H0
general nursery stock

William Dam Seeds
Highway 8
West Flamborough, Ontario L0R 2K0
untreated vegetable and flower seeds;
Canadian and European varieties

Downham Nursery, Inc.
626 Victoria Street
Strathroy, Ontario N7G 3C1

H.M. Eddie and Sons
4100 SW Marine Drive
Vancouver, British Columbia V7V 1N6
roses, general nursery stock

Flowers Canada
219 Silver Creek Parkway North
Unit 29
Guelph, Ontario N1H 7K4

251 Clark Street
Sherbrooke, Québec J1J 2N6

Gardeners and Florists Association of
Ontario
540 The West Mall No. 5
Etobicoke, Ontario M9C 1G3

Greenhedges
650 Montée de Liesse
Montréal, Québec H4T 1N8

Manitoba Nursery & Landscape
Association
104 Parkside Drive
Winnipeg, Manitoba R3J 3P8

McConnell Nurseries
R.R. 1
Port Burwell, Ontario N0J 1T0

Nursery Sod Growers' Association of
Ontario
Carlisle, Ontario L0R 1H0

Richters
Goodwood, Ontario L0C 1A0
herb seeds, esp. basil, gingseng seed

Saskatchewan Nursery Trades Association
c/o Harrison's Garden Centre
Box 460
Carnduff, Saskatchewan S0C 0S0

Sheridan Nurseries
700 Evans Avenue
Etobicoke, Ontario M9C 1A1

Greenhedges
650 Montée de Liésse
Montréal, Québec H4T 1N8

Glenpark
2827 Yonge Street
Toronto, Ontario M4M 2J4
perennials, roses, general nursery stock

Woodland Nurseries
2151 Camilla Road
Mississauga, Ontario L5A 2K1
rhododendrons, lilacs, azaleas

LANDSCAPE DESIGN ASSOCIATIONS

Alberta Association of Landscape
Architects
P.O. Box 3395
Station D
Edmonton, Alberta T5L 4J2

Association des Architects Paysagistes du
Québec
4003 Boul DeCarie
Suite 227
Montréal, Québec H4A 3J8

Atlantic Provinces Association of
Landscape Architects
c/o A. Bruce Martin
362 Saunders Street
Fredericton, New Brunswick E3B 1N9

British Columbia Society of Landscape
Architects
c/o The Registrar
115-2004 Mainland Street
Vancouver, British Columbia V6B 2T5

Canadian Society of Landscape Architects
P.O. Box 3304
Station C
Ottawa, Ontario K1J 4J5

Manitoba Association of Landscape
Architects
c/o Department of Landscape Architects
Faculty of Architecture
123 Bison Building
Winnipeg, Manitoba R3T 2N2

Ontario Association of Landscape
Architects
170 The Donway West
Suite 212
Don Mills, Ontario M3C 2G3

PUBLIC GARDENS

Butchard Gardens
Victoria, British Columbia

Dominium Arboretum
Ottawa, Ontario

Edwards Gardens
Toronto, Ontario

Humber Arboretum
Rexdale, Ontario

Montreal Botanical Garden
Montréal, Québec

Niagara Park Commission School of
Horticulture
Niagara Falls, Ontario

Queen Elizabeth Gardens
Vancouver, British Columbia

Royal Botanical Gardens
Hamilton, Ontario

SOURCES FOR FURTHER INFORMATION

Ministry of Agriculture
7000 113th Street
Edmonton, Alberta T6H 5T6

Ministry of Agriculture
80B Douglas Street
Victoria, British Columbia V8W 2Z7

Ministry of Agriculture
Rm. 165 Legislative Building
Winnipeg, Manitoba R3C 0V8

Ministry of Agriculture
801 Bay Street
Toronto, Ontario M7A 2B2

Ministry of Agriculture
P.O. Box 2000
Charlottetown, Prince Edward Island
   C1A 7N8

New Brunswick Ministry of Agriculture
P.O. Box 6000
Fredericton, New Brunswick E3B 5H1

Ministry of Agriculture
P.O. Box 1693
Québec, Québec J1R 4X6

Ministry of Agriculture
Walter Scott Building
Regina, Saskatchewan S4S 0B1

Ministry of Agriculture and Marketing
World Trade and Convention Center
Argyle Street
P.O. Box 1930
Nova Scotia B3J 2M4

BIBLIOGRAPHY

The American Society of Landscape Architects Foundation and the U.S. Dept. of Housing and Urban Development (H.U.D.) Office of Policy Development and Research. *Barrier Free Site Design*, Washington, D.C. 1977.

Brooks, John. *A Place in the Country*. London: Thames and Hudson, 1985.

Brooks, John. *The Small Garden*. New York: Van Nostrand Reinhold, 1978.

Brown, Emily. *Landscaping With Perennials*. Portland, Oreg: Timber Press, 1986.

Carpenter, Jot D., ed. *Handbook of Landscape Architectural Construction*. McLean, Va.: Landscape Architecture Foundation, 1976.

Cotton, Lin. *All About Landscaping*. San Francisco, Calif.: Ortho Books, 1980.

Church, Thomas. *Your Private World*. San Francisco, Calif.: Chronicle Books, 1969.

Douglas, Frey, et al. *Garden Design: History—Principles—Elements—Practice*. New York: Simon and Schuster, 1984.

Hanson, A.E. *An Arcadian Landscape: The California Gardens of A.E. Hanson 1920–1932*. Los Angeles, Calif.: Hennessey & Ingalls, 1985.

Hazlehurst, F. Hamilton. *Gardens of Illusion: The Genius of Andrew Le Nostre*. Nashville, Tenn.: Vanderbilt University Press, 1980.

Hillier Nurseries. *Hillier's Manual of Trees and Shrubs*. Great Britain: Redwood Burn Ltd., 1984.

Hobhouse, Penelope. *Color in Your Garden*. Boston: Little, Brown, 1985.

Itoh, Teiji. *Gardens of Japan*. Tokyo: Nissha Printing Co., 1984.

Jekyll, Gertrude, and Lawrence Weaver. *Gardens for Small Country Houses*. Great Britain: Antique Collector's Club, 1985.

Jekyll, Gertrude. *Wall and Water Gardens*. Salem, N.H.: The Ayer Company, 1983.

Jeannel, Bernard. *Le Notre*. Paris: Jean Mussot, 1985.

Staff of the L.H. Bailey Hortorium, Cornell University. *Hortus Third*. New York: Macmillan Publishing Co.

Paul, Anthony, and Yvonne Rees. *The Water Garden*. London: Penguin Books, 1986.

Pereire, Anita, and Gabrielle Van Zuylen. *Gardens of France*. New York: Harmony Books, 1983.

Reader's Digest Guide to Creative Gardening. London: Reader's Digest Association, 1984.

Schinz, Marina. *Visions of Paradise*. New York: Stewart, Tabori & Chang, 1985.

Sunset Books and *Sunset* magazine editors. *Sunset New Western Garden Book*. Menlo Park, Calif.: Lane Publishing Co., 1979.

Tolley, Emelie, and Chris Meade. *Herbs, Gardens, Decorations and Recipes*. New York: Clarkson N. Potter Publishers, 1985.

Verey, Rosemary. *The Scented Garden*. New York: Van Nostrand Reinhold, 1981.

Walker, Theodore D. *Site Design and Construction Detailing*. Mesa, Ariz.: PDA Publishers, 1978.

Weber, Nelva M. *How to Plan Your Own Home Landscape*. New York: Bobbs-Merrill Company, 1975.

INDEX